A Doryman's
D A Y

A Doryman's
DAY

Captain R. Barry Fisher

Tilbury House, Publishers 🏛 *Gardiner, Maine*
Maine Maritime Museum 🔱Ⓜ *Bath, Maine*

Tilbury House, Publishers
2 Mechanic Street
Gardiner, Maine 04345
800-582-1899
www.tilburyhouse.com

Maine Maritime Museum
243 Washington Street
Bath, Maine 04530
207-443-1316
www.bathmaine.com

First printing: June 2001

10 9 8 7 6 5 4 3 2 1

Cataloging-in-Publication Data

Fisher, R. Barry, 1928
    A doryman's day / R. Barry Fisher.
        p. cm
    ISBN 0-88448-233-2 (alk. paper)
        1. Fisher, R. Barry, 1928–2001. 2. Fishers—Massachusetts—
        Bibliography. I. title.

    SH20.F57 A3 2001
    639.2'092—dc21
    [B]   2001033048

Cover illustration: *Fishermen* by John Neville of Centreville, Nova Scotia, shows
alongshore dory fishing.

Book and cover designed on Crummett Mountain by Edith Allard, Somerville, Maine.
Layout by Nina DeGraff, Basil Hill Graphics, Somerville, Maine.
Editing and production by Jennifer Elliott and Barbara Diamond.
Scanning and film by Integrated Composition Systems, Spokane, Washington.
Printing and binding by Maple-Vail, Kirkwood, New York.

ON THE TITLE PAGE: Robert Barry Fisher in March, 1943, about the time he entered the
Merchant Marine at the age of fifteen.
Courtesy of R. Barry Fisher

Foreword

In the fall of 1995, after they came ashore from a season of running their Rockland, Maine, windjammer schooner HERITAGE, Captains Douglas and Linda Lee told all their friends about a remarkable storyteller who had sailed with them that summer. He lived in Newport, Oregon, but originated in Gloucester and was a professional fisherman (among other experiences, most on salt water). At the Lees' urging, I wrote to Captain R. Barry Fisher to invite him to speak at Maine Maritime Museum's annual Maritime History Symposium. As often as possible, we invite people to speak from their seafaring experience, as well as having scholars present the results of their research. Captain Fisher lived up to the Lees' promises. In May 1996, he delivered one of the most moving and informative presentations to which we have listened in (now) twenty-nine years of symposia.

The talk he gave that day is in this volume as the chapter "A Doryman's Day," somewhat further refined by himself. His passionate description of the life of a dory fisherman had the crowd salivating over his memories of the food served on the schooners, and shifting in their seats at his account of being cut by a swordfish. He left us all with lumps in our throats from his evident emotion at remembering his dorymates of decades ago, and the life lessons of his teenage years. Here was a man who loved being alive, who lived and remembered his life with an excitement and an emotional warmth that is rarely seen.

Barry Fisher was certainly the only man known to me who had gone dory trawling on the offshore Banks. Not only was he interested in talking about his experiences, he had a talent for storytelling and for making sense of the events and experiences of his life. In a letter to me in 1995, Barry had the following to say about the end of dory fishing: "The dory fishermen were doomed primarily because they could not get men at the end of the fishery. You could make from two-thirds to twice as much on a dragger catching the same amount of fish. For example, on the MARJORIE PARKER, we had ten or eleven dories and hence a total crew of twenty or twenty-two dorymen plus cook, engineer and captain. A Gloucester dragger of that period might have had a nine or ten man crew to catch the same amount of fish. Hence I think it's very important to point out that even though the dory fishermen, the vessels, made money—they turned a profit right to the very end—it was a lack of men that killed them. You can't blame the men, you can't blame the times. I would tell you that I never enjoyed a fishery ever again as much as I enjoyed dory fishing, but then of course I was only seventeen and eighteen years old, and a young fellow at that age is not the shiniest pistol in the box in terms of brain power. I never thought much about money. What I had, I spent and then it would be back to George's Bank for another withdrawal."

It wasn't just telling good stories to him—he was concerned with the meaning of it all, and trying to understand the Big Picture. Even in the formal context of his talk at our symposium, he included the all-encompassing rules for living which he had gotten from Captain Frank Hynes of the schooner MARJORIE PARKER and codified as "A Doryman's Legacy." You will read them at the end of the chapter, "A Doryman's Day."

At the time of his symposium talk, Captain Robert Barry Fisher sent me the following biography, which gives a quick overview of his life's adventure:

> Born 1928, Gloucester, Massachusetts. Lumped around the wharves from the age of eleven. Started going "catchee" on Gloucester vessels when I was fourteen. Sailed in the Merchant Marine 1943–45 to Africa, the Mediterranean countries, Northwest Europe, and the Soviet Union (Murmansk).
>
> 1946–50: Doryman on schooners, deckhand and mate on draggers out of Gloucester, Boston, and New Bedford, Massachusetts. 1950–53: U.S. Army, Korea—two full tours as a combat infantry-

man. 1954: Entered Harvard College on the strength of a general educational development certificate obtained in an army hospital while recovering from wounds. 1957–59: Timber cruiser in the Northwest and South America. 1959–60: Graduate School of Education, Harvard University. Received Master of Arts degree. 1960–63: Social Science teacher, Massachusetts and New Jersey.

1964: Returned to fishing—bought a 65-foot dragger and fished out of New Bedford. 1968: The vessel had burned and sunk and I accepted a post as Associate Professor of Fisheries at Oregon State University. Duties included teaching Commercial Fisheries to students, Fisheries Management to graduate students. Fifty percent of time spent on technology and gear development in the fleet (was the author of nine publications). Left the university in 1974. 1974–95: Owned and captained a succession of vessels from a 49-foot trawler to a 50 percent ownership in a 150-foot factory ship; also, two 87-foot midwater and bottom trawlers, and a 72-footer. During this period was continually involved in the testing and development of new trawl boards and trawl gear. Introduced pelagic or midwater trawling to the West Coast.

In 1978, in a cooperative effort between American catcher boats and Soviet processors, pioneered the joint ventures in the Pacific Northwest and in the Bering Sea. Over a twelve-year period our fleets produced 3,148,000 metric tons of finished product. I was the Senior American Fleet Captain in this fishery. I am also the only foreigner ever carried on the active duty rolls of the Soviet State Fishing Company, as a Master Mariner, and Senior Master Mariner and Navigator.

Of most importance, these joint ventures throughout the bitter years of the 1980s employed over 3,000 Russian men and women and American fishermen in a highly successful and profitable joint enterprise. The joint ventures grew to be the institution that broke the back of foreign domination of our fishing grounds in the Pacific Northwest and Alaskan waters. 1983–95: Involvement in a whole series of appointments to various groups involved with fishery management.

In 1985 re-appointed to the Oregon State University faculty as a Professor of Fisheries and I have currently served from that date to present as Chairman of the Coastal Oregon Marine Experiment Station of O.S.U.

Between 1995 and now, Barry spent a lot of time working on the writing of various parts of his life story. Besides the stories in this book, he wrote of his experiences in the Korean War, and started to put together the story of his time in the Merchant Marine, during World War II.

After the success of the symposium, Barry gave Maine Maritime Museum permission to publish the talk, and added a couple of other stories or chapters to it. The result is the book you hold in your hands. Although a purist might say the stories are not about Maine, we are proud to be presenting them, and we believe they have a lot to say about the New England fisherman of the mid-twentieth century and earlier. Also, we discovered that one of the vessels was actually owned in Maine at the time Barry sailed aboard, although he may not have known that fact.

This is Barry Fisher's book, and the words in it are all his. Maine Maritime Museum thanks the following people and institutions who have given us help in making his words into a book: Captains Douglas K. and Linda J. Lee; Erik A. R. Ronnberg, Jr.; Lynn-Marie Richard and Marven Moore at the Maritime Museum of the Atlantic in Halifax, Nova Scotia; Barbara Lambert and Ellen R. Nelsen at Cape Ann Historical Museum in Gloucester, Massachusetts; Earle R. (Bud) Warren; John Neville; Kathy M. Flynn at the Phillips Library, Peabody Essex Museum in Salem, Massachusetts; and Ralph D. Getson at Fisheries Museum of the Atlantic in Lunenburg, Nova Scotia. We deeply appreciate the friendly cooperation of Courtney Ellis Peckham of the Essex Shipbuilding Museum in Massachusetts. Her institution had a special relationship with Barry Fisher and might, if circumstances had been different, have ended up publishing this book. I offer special thanks to Jennifer Elliott, Edith

Allard, Barbara Diamond, Nina DeGraff and the other talented people who work for and with Tilbury House, without whom this book would have been lesser and much, much later.

As we neared the completion of preparations for this book, we were saddened to hear of Barry's declining health. On March 19th, 2001, we were stunned—though we had some warning—to learn that Barry had succumbed to cancer two days earlier. I, for one, thought of him as indestructible. I wish I could have asked him a last few questions, and that he could have seen this book in print. We are grateful to him for his teaching and storytelling abilities, and glad that he had what time he did to pass along the history he experienced, and some of life's lessons.

From his friends on the West Coast, especially Robert W. Schoning, Brad Warren, and Rod Moore, have come glowing accounts of his importance in their part of the world. He was valued as "one of the most respected fisheries leaders of his generation" and "a founder of the modern groundfish industry" (Warren). He was called a brilliant mentor and a natural leader for fishermen, government officials, and fisheries scientists alike. Members of all three groups, even including Russian fishermen from the "joint ventures" days, attended the memorial service for Captain R. Barry Fisher. He was legendary in his own time, a man hard to replace.

Fair winds, Barry, and thank you.

Nathan R. Lipfert
Library Director
Maine Maritime Museum
Bath, Maine

ROBERT BARRY FISHER
September 9, 1928 – March 17, 2001

Photo courtesy of R. Barry Fisher

Contents

A Doryman's
D A Y

A *Wharf Rat's* TALE

It seems to me I have always made some money as long as I was associated with the fishing industry, even when I was a young "wharf rat" in my hometown of Gloucester, Massachusetts, during the 1930s.

In those days, if a fisherman made $2,000 in a year he was not only on Easy Street, he was on the front pages of the *Gloucester Daily Times*. In order to make $2,000 he not only had to catch a helluva lot of fish, but he had to be able to sell them as well. Those were the days of the Great Depression, and some of my earliest memories were of seeing hundreds of thousands of pounds of good fish dumped into the harbor because there was no market. If a vessel tried to give away the fish to those who needed it—a couple of haddock or a codfish or two to take home—the cops were called by the fish plant owners to stop these gifts to hungry people; they claimed "free fish would ruin the market." What market? If a crew persisted in giving away free fish, they would get a "billy" bent over their heads.

There was no welfare system or unemployment checks in those days. From some back doors in Gloucester—doors not known or recognized by anybody but the wives with hungry children—the government did distribute flour, sugar, lard, dried beans, etc. On the days when these commodities were handed out, you wouldn't see any fishermen on "the corner." The Italians, Portuguese, "Boys from Home" (Newfoundlanders and Nova Scotians), and Yankees could not be seen anywhere on the street or in the pool halls or at the "Institute"—the Fishermen's Church Institute, with a game room, a reading room, and a grub bar, plus a dormitory upstairs for the "tranchers" (transients). All hands would be hiding for shame. The women going to accept hand-outs was harsh and candid proof that most fishermen and other workers could not "take care of their own." On that day they couldn't show their faces.

But even in those bad times we "wharf rats" had some money. After school we would run down to the docks to reel up gill nets on the large rotating gill-net reels that were reminiscent of the blades of a windmill. The gill nets in those days were made of linen thread, and the cork lines and the lead lines were of Manila and hung with cotton, all organic fibers which would soon rot unless cared for with more than a degree of patience. Each gill-net vessel had to have three "suits" of nets: one in the water soaking, another on the reels, and a third being taken out or brought back in from the sea.

We would reel up the gill nets for drying and then unreel and pack the already dried ones in shallow boxes on the decks of the vessels, which would leave at midnight or just after for the grounds. They would be back in and done by four or five in the afternoon, and the men would go home to eat supper and sleep.

A fasthanded wharf rat could make anywhere from thirty to sixty cents for three hours' work. Those were fair wages! It added up to two and sometimes three dollars a week. The boats didn't go out on Saturdays, so we were free to go to the "movin' picktchas."

Another source of income for enterprising wharf rats was to visit the larger vessels, the draggers or the schooners which were dory fishermen. The trick in this enterprise was to make known to a mate or cook your desire to work, without being obvious in displaying your presence and without getting underfoot. The penalty for the latter was an absentminded boot in the ass. We just stood around, hands in pockets, waiting for someone to yell, "Young fellah!"

Lots of times we would scrub down galleys and fo'c's'les or run errands for a cook. The cook would effect payment by yelling up to one of the crewmen, "Give this young fellah a half a dozen good haddock." A half-dozen haddock was always eight or nine. Sometimes we would also scrub pen boards, which were the boards used to partition the dressed and iced fish in the pens in the vessel's hold.

On a good vessel a couple of us could wash, scrub, rinse, and stack the pen boards neatly in three to four hours. Again, the pay would be half a dozen haddock or a couple of "chicken" halibut of ten to twenty pounds each. If you were working on a mackerel seiner, you'd probably get thirty or forty fat, beautifully hued "torpedoes"—blue and green silver-bellied Atlantic mackerel.

Most of us had what we called "soapboxes," which were homemade. To build one, a wharf rat had to make constant calls on the city dumps, the nearest of which was some four miles from the main part of town, to find a discarded baby carriage or toy wagon; there were precious few of these in the middle of the depression. Sometimes you had to go to the dump almost every day and twice on Sunday before you could get the four wheels and two axles with which to construct your soapbox. Then you had to get a couple of flat, strong boards about six feet in length and one foot wide. These boards were joined by crosspieces to brace them, and then the planks were fastened to the axle and wheels.

Next, you'd build a fish box to set on the rear of the vehicle. Scrap lumber for this was always available around the docks. You would bore a couple of drain holes in the bottom of the box and find yourself an old hunk of discarded sail canvas for a cover to protect the fish from flies or from a "bomb" from the gulls screaming and wheeling overhead.

The completed soapbox had a rope bridle on the front wheels so that you could haul the contraption around town. Some of the more enterprising wharf rats would paint "FISH" on the sides of the soapbox. The carts were always taken with us when we went down to the vessels to scrounge fish as payment for work. You had to be careful to hide the soapbox well in an out-of-the-way place near the docks, because otherwise some of the soapbox carts developed the ability to fly unaided.

The cook or a crewman would give you your fish, which had been put aside somewhere on the vessel for you. You would retrieve your soapbox, load the fish into the cart, and steal a couple of shovelfuls of ice from under the icehouses each plant had. About one time in ten, the plant foreman or some other asshole who was having a bad day would catch you scrounging ice.

BOY SAILING A DORY at Port Clyde, Maine, probably in the 1910s.

Sidney M. Chase photograph, Maine Maritime Museum

A Doryman's Day

They'd give you a cuff or two and boot your ass off the dock, a fair trade. If a foreman laid into wharf rats more frequently or with stronger kicks and cuffs, the vessel's cook or a doryman or sometimes even a skipper would allow it "warn't right to beat up a youngun' of nine or ten." A boot in the ass was educational and okay if a youngun' done wrong, but to hit a kid more than two or three times, "that warn't propah!" And the fisherman would look at the foreman or wharf worker with full measure and say, "You get my drift? You unnerstan'?"

Enough said. We would haul the soapboxes uptown and parade up and down the street peddling fish. Each group of kids had its own territory and territorial imperatives. The Italian kids patrolled the street near the Fort, the area where the Italian fishermen lived; the Portuguese kids had all the streets leading up to the "Portagee Hill"; the "English" kids, Yankees, Newfoundlanders, and Nova Scotians had the streets near the docks, in the central part of town.

The main shopping streets were shared by all on a first-come-first-served basis. We would march up and down the street peddling. The prices, as I best remember them, were ten or twenty cents for a prime "bull haddock" of eight to ten pounds, or we would get twenty-five cents for a fifteen-pound halibut. If the mackerel seiners were around, we would get forty or fifty cents for a dozen three-pound mackerel.

One time a priest at the Lady of Good Voyage Church, who was a fair hand at sketching and drawing, painted signs on both sides of the soapbox of a Portuguese kid's buggy. The pictures were of a schooner under full sail, with a sign in bright red and black letters which read, "MANUEL'S SEA FOOD EMPORIUM AND EXTRAVAGANZA!"

Holy Christ! Hot Diggety Damn! The furor that arose over that painted buggy was more intense than any Italian fisherman's four-day wedding party. Now we all had to deck out our buggies with identity, individuality, and style, or hide our heads in shame and be blown off the docks of Main Street, Gloucester Town!

That was my first encounter with the powers of artistic persuasion. Look out, Madison Avenue! Here come them "scrimy" wharf rats, each with his own advertising slogan. "FISHER'S FRESH FISH" was mine.

So you see, we always had money from selling fish or reeling gill nets or running errands, even though this was a time when lots of grown men had no coins to rub together in their pockets.

When I was about eleven years old, four of us had the chance to go "Big Time." We were waltzing around the docks one day on our customary patrols when Captain Wallace Walker, skipper of a fine dory vessel, asked us if we could use a dory. Beady little eyes perused him and waited for his next comment, because, you see, he had approached us first and begun the conversation. That went against the grain of every social custom on the waterfront. Skippers were big time; they were so exalted that you could even visualize them playing cribbage with God himself. Skippers never noticed wharf rats, and to speak to one first was simply never, never done. Finally, we said, "What do we want a dory for, Captain?" Captain Walker replied, "That be your business, t'ain't mine. But it seems to me as if some smart young fellahs had their own dory fit to go, well, they could maybe run a few lobster pots or a couple of skates of longline gear to catch black backs or yellowtails in the harbor, or maybe to get under the docks junking for scrap metal." (Black backs and yellowtails were flounder and sole, and scrap metal could be sold to the "junky man" for a quarter of a penny per pound.)

"Now boys," he said, "it just so happens that I had to condemn two dories, cause them young fellahs of mine on the vessel tell me they are too beat up for fishing in the ocean. Now if you young fellahs was to want them dories, you could help me get them up off the dock, out of the way, so to speak."

He hitched up his pants and looked up at the sky, which was what all fishermen did when an offer was being made or something serious was being proposed. He continued, "And maybe I could tell some young fellahs how to caulk her and brace her up and fit her out. We could scandalize frames and risers and planks from the other dory." (Scandalize, in Gloucester, meant to break something up for spare parts.) We looked at Captain Walker as if he were soft in the head or maybe had dipped into some of that demon black rum, 151 proof, that all of his Baptist brethren yelled about so much, so much that everyone, Baptist or no, had to investigate at least one time or more.

Captain Walker then spit a champion-sized gob of tobacco juice. We all looked at it lying in the street and realized that he was serious, because in those depression days in Gloucester, a fellah just couldn't be that free with tobacco juice unless he meant it.

Holy spit-whiskered Arabian Jaysus! It's for real! He means it! It was a good thing the priest wasn't around to hear this blasphemy. Baptist captains were allowed to swear once or twice. Captain Walker, being a good Baptist, didn't hold much with Papists, which was a term still used by strong Protestants looking down their blue-frozen fine noses at Catholics. We learned later from Captain Walker that there were a couple of other titles he used to describe Catholics, such as "knee-bending mackerel snappers" or "genuflecting guppy-gulpers" or "mendacious minnow munchers."

It should be said right now that humorous theologically based wisecracks thrown at each other were the cement which bound together the Catholics, Baptists, Methodists, Universalists, and the Congregationalists in Gloucester. None of us would have been able to handle the Unitarians, but of course they weren't part of the fishing industry. Fishing was a hard, cruel, mean way of life, and a fisherman's faith had to be prominent, vivid, and strong. No Unitarians and no Church of England—by those standards—need apply. Back to the dory.

Under Captain Walker's direction we got a bunch of rollers and horsed the two dories up off the dock to a spare bit of unused landfill. Captain Walker allowed as that was work enough for one day. And if we didn't have nothing to do, he would meet us about eight o'clock the next morning, which was Saturday. He left to go home for supper. We weren't satisfied; we raced around, got old boxes and some dory paint, and made up big signs to circle the two dories. "No Trespassing or any other kind of Assing. KEEP OFF. STAY OUT. You are being Watched."

We were all down by the dories by 7:25 AM waiting for Captain Walker. We waited some more. By five minutes to eight we were convinced that Captain Walker wouldn't show. He had pulled a fast one on us, he had. He'd gulled us into helping him dispose of the two dories, which he no longer needed aboard the schooner CORINTHIAN.

The town clock struck eight bells, and on the second stroke of the bell Captain Walker came into view around the corner, driving hard, hands in pockets, and with a greeting of, "Good morning to you, young fellahs. Good morning. Glad to see you're on time."

Then he let go with something else that took us aback. "I see the KILLARNEY is in; let's go find out how Carl done this trip. Timmy Foote is cook with him, and that man turns out good doughnuts. Let's go and get a mug-up and get the news." (A mug-up was a snack.)

"What about the dories?" I asked.

Captain Walker fixed me a look of mild reproof. "They were there all night, they are there now, and they'll be there after we get our mug-up. Come along now, you."

After a good mug-up on the KILLARNEY and watching Captain Carl Olsen and Captain Walker having a too-long conversation about the weather and the Boston Red Sox and fish and the chances and dangers that would accompany the Gloucester High School football team that season, we came back to the dories.

Captain Walker then said, "Any of you young fellahs got any coins? You'll need some scratch for caulking or putty or nails to fasten her up with."

We immediately pooled our resources, and we were, at that

BOYS AT PORT CLYDE, Maine, with their dory, a decade or two before
Barry Fisher and his friends had theirs.

Sidney M. Chase photograph, Maine Maritime Museum

point, short of much in the way of liquid assets. After a quick meeting of the partners-to-be in that dory we replied, "No, Captain, we ain't got much money."

Captain Walker rolled his cud from one cheek to another and said, "Well, boys, get a hold onto me when you got the coin. One of them two dories is bound to be your own rebuilt dory. You see, if I was to come up with the scratch for your dory, 'twouldn't be right, 'cause, you see, anything you get for nothin' ain't worth nothin'. Unnerstan' me? Get my drift?" And he turned around and went downwind, down the street.

For three weeks we raised capital. We sold our four soapbox buggies. That was a hard stunt to pull off. All the other wharf rats along the five-and-one-half-mile Gloucester waterfront would get awfully inquisitive if four buggies were being sold sudden-like at one time. So we sold one down in East Gloucester; another to an Italian kid down at the Fort, four miles away; and we lent out the other two to kids on shares. Next, we called in some old favors and loans we had made, meantime avoiding wharf rats whom we owed. We even sold good collections of bubblegum baseball-player cards and prime agates, marbles, and nooggies. The Harvard Business School couldn't have done better. Even after these Herculean sacrifices we felt we didn't have enough money to outfit the dory. We decided to float some loans, if possible, from our fathers.

I went to Dad and asked him to lend me $2.50. Dad wanted to make this a true business enterprise with terms, interest, and all that bullshit. I had never realized before that money had such a big anchor on it to keep it firmly under the control of the person who owned it. The old man taught me good, right then and there, that to borrow money means you get a piece of that anchor to lug around with you, known as interest, and it ran like a no-rundown clock all the time. The $2.50 was principal. The whole thing was called a mortgage.

Years later when I read about the Mafia and all their business connections, I then understood my father, the only Yankee gentleman I ever knew who could have been a Mafia don. I dimly understood that my father was also of the same class as Captain Wallace Walker: "Anythin' you get for nothin' ain't worth nothin'."

We ended up with $19.16 — or was it $16.19? I can't recall which. But that was more than a week's pay for the majority of the adult males of Gloucester in those times. Captain Walker took us around to a couple of ship chandler's shops. He picked out and explained the purchases we were making. We needed cotton, oakum, and caulking putty to "pay the seams" in the dory's floor planking and her side strakes. We needed galvanized nails to fasten the planking and frames. We needed a small bit of rope for painters and beckets. We needed oars and tholepins. We needed dory anchors and some anchor line.

But the money ran out. We didn't have enough for a spritsail or paint or fishing gear or a compass. It was the spritsail and compass we wanted most. With a sail and compass we could lay courses and make our "drift good" along with all the other great navigators, even if Gloucester Harbor was almost totally landlocked. The chandler told us our credit was good and that he'd "cuff us." Captain Walker let go with a snort that sounded midway between a fart and coughing up a lunger. He jerked his head at us, signaling for a meeting outside. The chandler's door closed behind us, and we followed the captain around the corner out of sight.

"Boys," he said, "don't ever go on credit. These conniving bastards that live shoreside are always throwing credit at you. All your life they'll throw credit at you. Credit is something the devil thought up. It was dreamed up by Satan himself. I'm telling you, young fellahs, don't ever buy nothing on credit. And even worse, don't never lend or borrow from a friend. Now one of you boys go back in and tell that sonovabitch, 'Thank you sir, but we'll be back when we have the coin.'"

We did that. It took us several weeks of conniving to raise enough money to outfit the dory with gear. Captain Walker then showed us how to caulk seams, how to put in new frames, how

THE WARVES OF GLOUCESTER. The schooner in the foreground is
probably the ROB ROY, which lasted from 1900 to 1918.

Sidney M. Chase photograph, Maine Maritime Museum

A Doryman's Day

to replank the dory where necessary, and how to recap the gun-wales. We painted her up good, burnt-orange with green gunwale caps. We made kid-boards which, when placed thwartships would make a pen for the fish and keep them out from underfoot.

We needed something else, though. We invited the priest down, him of "Manuel's Seafood Emporium and Extravaganza" fame. Looking up at the clouds, with my hands in my pockets, I asked him would he be good enough to paint on both the dory's bow planks the name THE FOUR BROTHERS, and on both sides of her stern, her hailing port, Gloucester. He allowed as how he would if we would get him the paint, and he'd give the dory his blessing for free if we would bring him a couple of good fish or maybe a lobster or two when we got going.

Lenny was a somewhat suspicious type, more than the rest of us. He looked at Captain Walker and said, "Ain't that credit, Captain?"

"No, young fellah, that's what they call a contract. Father has got something he will do for you now, and then you'll feed him a time or two, and that's fair and square."

Lenny didn't believe it. He always was stubborn, and he always remembered nits. "But, Captain, he—" His toes got stepped on hard. The captain and the priest got laughing, and Father Perry said, "He's right, boys. It's a contract." Lenny got some hard looks, and he didn't say a word.

Captain then said, "Listen to Father Perry, boys. He is a man of God, a man of the cloth; he don't lie. And even if he is a Catholic, don't hold that against him. I'm a Baptist, and even I don't hold that against him." Then Father Perry and Captain Walker got laughing like hell and slapped each other on the shoulder. It was just foolishness!

Well, we got the FOUR BROTHERS going good. Captain Walker had us get all the gear we needed for dory trawling: buoys, buoy anchor lines, trawl anchors, ground lines, ganging lines, and hooks to catch black-back flounder, codfish, and yellowtail flounder in the harbor. He showed us how to rig the gear and fish it.

We discovered that the best place in the harbor to fish was right outside of the sewer outfall. All of the flounder from that spot were extra fat. We fixed the exact position of the sewer outfall by lining up the "ranges"—buildings and trees on shore— which when they were lined up just right on intersecting angles and laid out by compass point, fixed our position. That was my first lesson in dead-reckoning navigation. We told our customers only that we had a real good spot for flounder and codfish.

Lenny's uncle was a lobsterman, and he showed us how and helped us to rebuild about twenty-five junker lobster traps. He gave us some tips on how lobsters moved and what they were like in the moon phases and tide runs. He taught us well. A lobster to him wasn't just an animal. It was a "being" with needs and appetites, a part of the web of life, and lobsters deserved respect.

He and Captain Walker went shares with us. We owed each one of them 15 percent of all that we made on longline trawl gear or the lobster pots for one calendar year. That wasn't credit, either. That was shares. (Shuddup, Lenny.) All the money we made junkin' scrap metal out from under the docks at low tide was ours, at a cent a pound for copper and brass and a quarter of a cent a pound for iron or steel. The pickings were pretty good because there weren't any other kids in town that we knew of who had a dory.

The following summer we rigged up a haul seine and caught "turd" pollock—juvenile fish about two years old—for lobster bait, when they gathered under the fish offal pipes from the fish-filleting houses. We got seventy-five cents for a sugar barrel holding 140 pounds. We had a full year, the finest kind of season. We were dorymen, and we acted like dorymen, cocky little buggers. Lots of the wharf workers and the fishermen may have laughed at us, but they treated us dead-serious-like.

We always had a couple of bucks apiece in our pockets, and in those days the movie house on Saturday afternoon had a special for kids. These movies were at least three chapters of Flash Gordon or Tom Mix or Buck Rogers or Tarzan, followed by some kind of sports short, and an action movie, plus two cartoons. The price was fifteen cents in the orchestra or ten cents in the balcony or the rear of the theater. Popcorn was a nickel a bag. They had penny candy (five to ten pieces of candy for a penny) and tonic (Gloucester talk for soda pop), which was three cents a glass for one squirt of syrup or five cents for two squirts). The Four Brothers always ordered, "Let come your double barrel, sweeten 'er up."

We were the lords of creation, standing our luckless or broke friends to candy or a tonic, just like the good dorymen did in the taverns. If you dared, and knew you wouldn't get found out, you'd sneak some candy to a girl, a certain girl. Girls in those days wore thick black or tan cotton stockings, and their dresses were mostly homemade, some with lace collars or wrist trim. Some were made of hundred-pound flour sacks printed in bright patterns. The labels printed on them would wash out after a couple of tubbings.

You'd sneak that girl a treat or two, maybe by way of a neutral friend, and then maybe you got a chance to buy her an ice-cream soda at a soda fountain well removed from the movie house. The intermediaries of these intrigues were always carefully selected. No young doryman could afford being labeled as a young fellah interested in girls. The intermediaries were sworn to secrecy by death-and-blood oaths.

You never knew exactly why you wanted to make these meetings. Sometimes you could feel it in your gut, a strange, pulling compulsion, or sometimes you started sweating hard. We all knew all there was to know about "boys will be boys and girls will be girls," but none of us knew the how's and why's of it. It was a strange feeling. I knew about salmon and how they mated, and I was always staggered by the fact that when it came time for them to do it, then they had to die. We thought we knew what boys and girls were about, but in those days nobody ever told you anything. We recognized that the older dorymen and fishermen acted like goddamn fools around girls, so we knew there was something to the whole thing. And at times, the anxious little grin or the gracious curl of a girl's hair was enough to turn you into a drunken bear cub, clumsy with eagerness and stuck in not knowing what came next.

Life was good for us then. We had plenty of coin. We could buy baseballs new, and didn't ever have to use balls lopsided from use and carefully wrapped with black friction tape because the horsehide cover was long gone. These were dead when they hit the ash of a bat.

There came a day when we were twelve years old when we went down to the docks to go fishing. The CORINTHIAN was in from a trip with a good load of fish. We went down to say good morning to Captain Walker. He wasn't there, but the cook yelled up at us, "Come down, boys, the grub's on. Fresh tea. Come get a mug-up, you dorymen." We swung aboard via the rigging and went down into the galley in the forepeak of the vessel.

The cook, Jim Eustes, had a mug of black tea steaming and a big slice of mince pie waiting for each of us. Jim was a "herring choker," a "boy from home," a Newfoundlander. Jim was famed in the fleet for his stews and chowders, his boiled dinners, his salt-fish feeds, his pies and cakes, and his lad-in-the-bag (steamed duff pudding made with dark molasses, raisins, and lots of dates and quinces, served with a hard rum sauce). His biscuits and dumplings were rich in their exquisite flakiness. Dorymen followed Jim from vessel to vessel. When "Jim was cook with you," life on that vessel was a constant "bait up of good grub." His smoked-shoulder dinners with boiled vegetables and red-flannel hash would have made it into *Bon Appetit* or any other gourmet magazine.

Jim kept refilling the mugs of tea from his spotless blue enamel "tea b'iler." "Go at it, me sons. Go at it good, boys. Now's your chance to fill and empty the plates. All you get out of this life is a good feed now and then, and a rag or two, some stylish, some not, just a rag to cover your back. Maybe a good drink or two or a dance or a fight or two. So eat up. Eat up good, boys. How ye makin' out, me darlin's? How's the dorying goin'? I hear tell that

THE FOUR BROTHERS is a highliner in Gloucester Harbor."

Jim was also known as a "motor mouth." He sang a passable tenor and was a grand fiddler, but Lord God, he was a good gammer! A gammer was a storyteller, a man who could recite endless verses of the oral epics that were the doryman's poetry. And the ghost stories, ah, the ghost stories: "The FLYING DUTCHMAN," "The Wreck of the HESPERUS," "The Tales of the MARY CELESTE." Jim knew them all, and he could hold a gang of men hanging with the music of his voice and the tallness of the tale as if he were the Pied Piper himself. Ah, Jim Eustes, he knew them all.

And he knew Robert Service and Jack London, too. He even knew some Longfellow and Walt Whitman, and that made him the finest kind of gammer, because Jim couldn't read or write, you know. He knew numbers well enough, but he was no reader. If a new song or story had to be learned Jim would have the reader read it over to him, and he would repeat, and repeat, word by word, and then he'd "have her down."

I asked, "Where's your fiddle, Jim?" I was hoping to lead him into the playing of a jig or a reel, a schottische or a strathspey. Jim just shook his head. "No, today's not a day for the playing of the fiddle. Here, boys, try these doughnuts." He poured us more tea, strong and black, primed with brown sugar and evaporated milk.

Just as we were finishing the doughnuts we heard a sob; someone was crying. In those days and on those vessels, tears from a man were a rare thing. Jim motioned us to follow him up the ladder and onto the deck. We walked aft with him and he sat himself down on the cabin's trunk. He called us close and put his arms around us. "You know," he said, "that's Stan, boys, that's Stan crying. The old man, Captain Wallace, he went up to town to sell the trip. The priest met him and gave him a letter from down home [Newfoundland]. Stan's Da' and his three brothers are gone, gone in a gale, the vessel lost; a hard blow, me sons, a hard blow for a fine Christian lad like Stan. His Ma and one young sister are left."

Oh, Lord Jaysus, none of us knew what to do. Then we were all crying, Jim too. "Come near, me sons, come near; give us a hug, boys. A hug, sometimes it helps, often it don't. I thought maybe if you young fellahs had come aboard and ate, it would help drive the black away. You know, the cold and black that comes with despair and dying."

But it didn't.

"Oh God, You are the Way, the Resurrection, and the Life. You give, and You take, and that's fair and square. It's just that sometimes, Lord, You hit some awful hard licks. It's not for the likes of me to squawk or shirk, but You left only Stan and his Ma and the girl. That's a cruel, hard lick, Lord, a cruel, hard lick."

We were as stones. The grub in our bellies was like cannon balls, leaden and so heavy as to pull us down to the deck. Jim blew his nose on his apron and turned to us. "Me sons, have you got any coin on you? If you do, go buy some flowers. Go to the church. Light some candles, and leave the flowers at the feet of the Blessed Virgin. Ask Father Perry to say a Mass for Stan's Da' and his brothers, and give him some coin for the Mass and the poor. Save a couple of flowers for to give to Stan.

"Come back and tell Stan about the candles and Mass. He'll like that; he'll like that grand. Then when you've given the flowers he'll understan' that it's just like us, it is. A flower is born, and it sprouts, and the leaves come, just like us, growing and branching out. The buds come then, and then the flowers, the petals that catch the sun. They triumph in beauty, and then they fall. Then that flower dies, just like us, it is.

"But we'll tell Stan about the flowers, we will, tell him that if a plant is cared for it goes on bringing flowers for a long time. Now away with you, away with you all. You've men's work to do. This is all part of being a doryman, but mind you, come back and tell Stan, and bring him his flowers. He'll be here, in his bunk."

We didn't go fishing that day. We did what Jim told us to do, and we came back with some flowers. I believe it was the first time we'd ever bought flowers on our own. We came back to the vessel, and Stan was out of his bunk, talking quiet-like and holding hands with Jim. Stan thanked us, and we all held hands with him for a long time. Then Jim yelled at us, "Fresh turnovers, boys! Clear a place! Fresh tea, too. Mug-up time." Jim was never what you would call quiet-like.

"Now Stan, you and me will go partners, and we'll beat the be-Jaysus out of these young dorymen. Get out the crib board, Stan, and the cards." We played cribbage for a long spell. We ate all of the turnovers together, and they were good.

The next day we went fishing. The day after that we were hauling trawl lines. It was misty in the harbor. The KILLARNEY slipped up on us out of the patchy fog. The gang was running up her mainsail. They had already swayed the foresail and fore staysail onto her. She was slipping by close-hauled on a starboard tack.

Captain Wallace Walker was at the helm. He looked us over, hitched his head around, and let go with a big spray of tobacco juice in our direction. Stan was at the mainsail sheet, snugging it down.

"Luck, Stan," we yelled.

"Luck, young fellahs. Luck."

A Doryman's
DAY

I was a dory fisherman on two schooners, the MARJORIE PARKER of Boston and the ROBERTSON II of Shelburne, Nova Scotia, in 1946 and 1947.

In these schooners I fished primarily at what was called "shacking"—catching cod and haddock and limited amounts of pollock, cusk, and hake for the fresh-fish market. I also made one trip line-trawling for halibut in the ROBERTSON II.

Both vessels were classic schooners, but they both had been built with engines as the main propulsion and carried an abbreviated sail plan. However, in hull shapes and lines they were true schooners.

I won't spend any time describing the schooners. Better hands and voices than mine have written masterfully of the American fishing schooners, which unfortunately reached their peak in performance and speed just as they were replaced by the irrefutable business logic of diesel-powered trawlers. When I was young, there were still schooners around in Boston and in Gloucester, and as I saw them come and go, it was almost always with a wish or a dream that I could be on them. In my fantasies I was everything from a fore-top masthead man high aloft laughing with the gods, to a skipper lashed to the open helm of a great schooner in a storm.

The dories these schooners carried were nested in cradles in the vessel's waist, port and starboard, between the foremast and mainmast. The dories were ingenious craft—simple in concept and construction, but ideally suited to their function.

I had a keen appreciation of the dories, I think, because not only could I sense the workings and relationships of dories, tubs of longline trawl gear, and schooner, but also because a dory, in my imagination, was something that I and other eight or nine year olds could handle right then and there if given half a chance.

Double-banked dories had been a part of my life from the time when I became a "wharf rat" hanging around the docks in Gloucester, Massachusetts, where I was born. In the mid to late

DORY TRAWLER SADIE M. NUNAN, built at East Boothbay, Maine, in 1901. This photograph was taken after 1915, when she had an engine installed. The photographer was a Portland pilot who took the picture as the NUNAN was coming out of Portland. Although she has all her lower sails set, you can also see the engine exhaust behind her transom. Stacks of dories can be seen on her deck, and the sharp-eyed observer can also see the mast caps which would permit the rigging of topmasts. The NUNAN is probably seen here with a reduced winter rig. She was converted to a yacht in 1939.

Charles Sayle Collection, Maine Maritime Museum

A Doryman's Day

NESTED DORIES on the deck of a Boston schooner, c. 1920.

Sidney M. Chase photograph, Maine Maritime Museum

1930s there were still a few vessels whose owners had stubbornly resisted converting to dragging.

A dory's size was measured by the length of her bottom, not the length overall. If a dory was said to be fifteen feet, that meant her length on bottom was fifteen feet but her length overall was nineteen feet because of the overhang of bow and stern. Dories were built to carry fish, to be rugged and seaworthy, capable of nesting one inside the other on the schooner's deck, and they had to be cheap.

Their lapstrake planks on the sides and a rockered bottom promoted seaworthiness, allowing the dories to be lifted by on-coming waves. They had great sheer, with high bows and sterns, and they had good flare outwards on the sides. This resulted in a

FULLY RIGGED DORY, ready for a two-tub set.
Illustration by Jill Pridgeon

A Doryman's Day

boat that became more and more seaworthy as she was loaded, and gave her improved handling characteristics under either oar or sail. The dories were double-ended, which added to their seaworthiness, either going into the wind and the sea or running from them. In the stern of each dory there was a hole which was left unplugged when the dories were aboard to promote drainage while nested in their cradles. When they were rigged for fishing, a hardwood plug was driven into the hole. This plug had a length of $\frac{1}{4}$-inch-diameter Manila line passed through a hole bored in the plug, and the line extended into a loop made by an eye splice that was approximately 15 to 18 inches long. If a dory capsized, her dorymen would be able to hang onto the loop of the line while waiting rescue.

DORY LONG LINE showing the parts.

Illustration by Jill Pridgeon

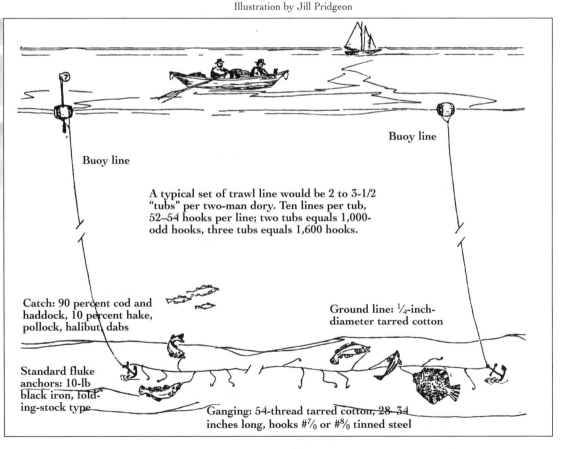

A typical set of trawl line would be 2 to 3-1/2 "tubs" per two-man dory. Ten lines per tub, 52–54 hooks per line; two tubs equals 1,000-odd hooks, three tubs equals 1,600 hooks.

Catch: 90 percent cod and haddock, 10 percent hake, pollock, halibut, dabs

Ground line: $\frac{1}{4}$-inch-diameter tarred cotton

Standard fluke anchors: 10-lb black iron, folding-stock type

Ganging: 54-thread tarred cotton, 28–34 inches long, hooks #$\frac{7}{0}$ or #$\frac{8}{0}$ tinned steel

Buoy line

Buoy line

The dories were universally painted an orange-buff color (which weathered very well), oftentimes with dark-green cap-rails. Each dory had a number and this was painted on the bow, a black numeral on top of a white circle or simply the black numeral, about ten inches high.

Now for the gear. The trawl gear of a dory schooner was quite simple. It was relatively inexpensive, it was easy to build, and it could be maintained well during the fishing operation. The gear consisted of two buoys and two buoy lines which went from the buoy to one of two anchors that held the trawl or the long-line on the bottom. Tied between these two anchors was a very long ground line. Each line in this gear was 55 fathoms long. The lines were made of $\frac{1}{4}$-inch-diameter tarred-cotton line. Each line had a 15- to 18-inch loop tied at each end. These connected lines were tied from the anchor, one onto another, until all the gear was set. The other end was tied onto the other anchor buoy line.

Along each line gangings or branch lines were tied every six feet. The gangings varied in length from 27 to 32 inches. On the end of each ganging there was a loop tied and this loop was used to secure a number $\frac{7}{0}$ or $\frac{8}{0}$ tinned-steel codfish hook.

The ground lines or trawl lines, as said before, were connected one to the other; ten of these lines, each holding fifty-two or fifty-three gangings with their hooks was a "tub of trawl." All references to the fishing gear were always made in terms of "it was a two-tub set" or "we set three tub!" This meant that three tubs would have thirty lines set between the anchors.

The buoy lines led up from the gear and were tied to two buoys. These buoys were made of 100-pound nail kegs, and they were painted and strapped so that buoy lines could be made fast to them. The weather or windward buoy was called a "high flier" because it carried a flag staff protruding up from the buoy's center; the other end of the staff protruded from the buoy's bottom and was weighted with chain. At the top of the roughly 4 $\frac{1}{2}$-foot staff, a round wire ring was lashed. A piece of light canvas was sewed to the round wire ring and the canvas carried the dory's number. The other buoy, or the downwind or leeward buoy, did not have a "high flier." It was simply a painted and strapped 100-pound nail keg with the dory's number painted on each end.

As gear was made up or when it was coiled in the dory, it was always handled in the same manner. The doryman would quickly make three or four small loops of the ground line in one hand, run his free hand down the ganging to the hook, place the hook over the loops that his other hand held, and then drop these loops and hook into a trawl tub. The trawl tubs that carried all of the trawl lines were made of light hardwood (I've forgotten what kind) and were held together with either metal strapping or tough hardwood withes (or bands). The tubs were approximately 30 to 32 inches high with a diameter of some 26 or 28 inches. There were two holes set 4 or 5 inches apart at the top of the tub. Facing these were another two holes on the other side. Lengths of half-inch Manila rope were roved and tied through the holes as straps or handles and served both to keep the trawls in the tub and as lifting straps for handling the trawl tub.

I should describe the clothes we wore, our sleeping accommodations, and a few words about personal hygiene (of which there wasn't much). The fo'c's'les of the dory schooners were huge. They had to be to accommodate both the galley and the large number of crewmen in a dory vessel. The galley was at the after part of the fo'c's'le, with a large coal-burning stove usually placed athwart ship just behind the companionway. There was a long dresser or working counter on top of a waist-high cabinet along the after bulkhead, which faced the stove. This dresser was the principal place upon which the cook prepared his foods. The cupboards below held pots and pans. On the starboard side an insulated icebox was built in, and on the after side of the icebox was the forward bulkhead of the fish hold. There was a small sliding door cut in this bulkhead, through which ice could be readily passed into the galley icebox.

Drinking water and water for dishes was obtained from a cast-iron hand pump at one side of the dresser. The schooners did not carry much water, so every drop was cared for. There was a bucket under the spout of the cast-iron pump to catch any spill water. This bucket also filled a deep, two-compartment rectangular sink made of galvanized sheet metal, which was hung from the side rails on the stove. The two compartments were filled with water and soap and served to wash and rinse all the dishes and pots and pans. A hot water boiler—a high, oblong pot with an eight- to ten-gallon capacity—was on the stove at all times. Anyone needing hot water could dip into this container, but there was an iron rule: If you took a cup of hot water out, you replaced it from cold water from the pail. Another iron rule required all of us to wash and clean our mugs, any eating utensils used, and the spot where we ate when we had a mug-up.

Others rules prevailed. The cook was probably the hardest working and most appreciated man on the vessel. All dorymen went out of their way to do little chores for the cook, such as carrying up and emptying his slop pails, making sure he had a good supply of kindling to start his coal fires on the stove, cleaning up around the table, and sweeping or mopping down for him. The cook generally was also the vessel's first-aid man, and as such was often called Doc or Doctor. He was the uncontested boss of the fo'c's'le.

A little anecdote illustrates the cook's primacy aboard a dory schooner. In the mid 1930s, a captain who was one of the greatest moneymakers of all time found himself short one dory in his crew and asked a couple of good dorymen if they would like to go with him. The answer came after a short period of hands stuck in the pockets and all three men eyeing the sky. "Ahhh, who be cook with ya, boy?"

Food was not only kept in the icebox, but also iced down in the fish holds and was drawn upon as the cook needed it. Lockers and cupboards ran up the sides of the fo'c's'le. A mug-up locker was kept full of snack food: coldcuts, cheese, butter, sugar, canned milk, bread, pastry, molasses, sardines, etc.

A Doryman's Day

A narrow table butted against the foremast ran forward into the peak of the fo'c's'le. This long table had two long, wedge-shaped drop leaves which were held in place with hooks and chains when the table was laid.

On one side of the fo'c's'le was a deep open locker in which oilskins were hung to dry. Running forward from the lockers on both sides were top and bottom bunks that lined the inner sheathing of the schooner. There were generally at least five pairs of bunks on each side in the fo'c's'le. It was common in vessel fo'c's'les that some of the top bunks were double bunks with a board in-between, where you slept with your dorymate. Every bunk had a shelf built along the sheathing in which you stowed your gloves, nippers, tobacco, reading material, dittybag, etc. Boots were stowed beneath the bottom bunks throughout the fo'c's'le. There were long continuing lockers just in front of the bunks, running on each side up into the eyes of the vessel, which served not only as seats at the dining table, but also as lockers for stowing staples and other food items.

More men slept aft in the vessel's cabin. There were two single bunks for the skipper and the engineer. There were also at least two double bunks in which two dorymen slept, again separated by a board. In those days and in those vessels, fishermen provided their own mattresses, pillows, and bedding. Bedding consisted usually of two good-quality wool blankets or quilts, a pillow, and a pillowslip made from the bags that 50 pounds of flour came in. The latter were all brightly printed, but the printed words would fade out after two or three washings.

We dressed pretty much the same winter and summer: long underwear, wool pants, a heavy flannel shirt underneath, and a wool shirt on top. The sleeves of all shirts were "staked"—the cuffs were cut off completely and the sleeves cut back so that the end of the shirt sleeve came to about mid forearm. This was done to prevent boils and sores caused by fish slime and sand in the cuff of your shirt. The sleeves of our oil jackets did rub our wrists, but you could keep those washed off. A lot of dorymen wore two or three turns of brass or copper chain around their wrists. The sulfides in the metal were an antidote against infections caused by fish slime.

In the wintertime we would usually add one flannel shirt, again worn under the wool shirt. Our feet were covered by two pairs of thick wool socks or one pair of socks and sheepskin boot moccasins. Boots were bought two sizes too big so that they could be kicked off easily if you went overboard. In the winter a great many men wore wool scarves, wool face masks, and wristers. Mittens were worn with a lanyard that passed from one mitten, up the sleeve of your oil jacket, across your back, and down the other jacket sleeve to the other mitten. This way mittens could be quickly taken off and not lost. Head wear was generally a railroad engineer's cotton cap in summer and a woolen hunting cap with visor and earmuffs in winter.

Our oilskins were oiled "skins"—linen suits that had been treated with shellac and fish oil mixed in. They and the sou'westers we wore had to be thoroughly cleaned and repainted every couple of months. With luck you might get a year out of a suit of oilskins. They stunk. You couldn't let them get too hot in the fo'c's'le or they would stick together; if they got too cold, they would freeze and crack on you. The early rubber-coated "oilskins" were too heavy and too expensive for wear. There were no synthetics.

Now let's turn to personal hygiene aboard the schooners. There was almost none, so it's an easy topic. The leeward rail and the old oaken draw bucket took care of bodily excretions. The schooners did not carry sufficient water, so the only time that you washed was when you washed and shaved on the way in. Otherwise hands and faces were washed from the saltwater hoses on deck. Generally teeth were brushed only on the way into port. Because of this lack of care and diet, most dorymen had lost all or most of their teeth by their mid thirties.

Now, let me describe how the fishery worked. On a typical day, winter or summer, the crew was called approximately two hours before dawn. The cook would have been up for probably at least one hour by this time getting his baking started, and he would have fresh coffee and tea on the coal-burning stove.

There would be little conversation. The skipper would have passed forward the order of how many tubs of trawl to bait, and the crew would hurriedly slurp down their tea and coffee, perhaps with a piece of bread or a muffin. Oilskins would be grabbed from the oilskin lockers both forward in the fo'c's'le or in the cabin aft where some of the dorymen lived. All hands turned out on deck.

Some of the "hold men" (men who worked in the fish hold icing the fish) would already have broken out the main hatch covers and would begin to fill and pass up the hardwood bait buckets full of frozen herring and/or mackerel to the waiting dorymen on deck. These were the standard baits. In earlier times, clams had also been used. The frozen mackerel or herring had been taken from cold storage prior to leaving port. Canvas was spread in the wing pens where the frozen bait was kept with a foot or two of ice under the canvas. The bait was put in the pen and then covered with another piece of canvas and a heavy layer of ice was placed on top. Bait thus handled would be in a frozen or semi-frozen state for five to seven days.

The bait was used carefully. It was stood on its head, your hand holding the tail, and then with a bait knife you sliced down along the belly side toward the head. The two pieces together were placed side by side on a cutting board and you chopped away the head. Then you chopped these halves so as to get about twelve to sixteen usable pieces of bait. The tails and the heads were discarded. Four to six herring or mackerel were needed to bait one line of gear.

Baiting would go on all over the after part of the vessel. There were cutting stages or boards which were placed in cleats

LOADING ICE on a fishing schooner at Boston, c. 1920.

Sidney M. Chase photograph, Maine Maritime Museum

A Doryman's Day

CUTTING BAIT and baiting trawl lines on a Boston schooner. Note the tubs of trawl line in the foreground; one is baited, with the baited hooks arranged around the rim of the tub.

Sidney M. Chase photograph, Maine Maritime Museum

on the cabintop, and men ringed three sides of the cabin. Baiting was also done in the fish hold. Both vessels I was on had some electric lights in pigtail receptacles made up on a line in the hold, but these had to be augmented by candles in the fish hold for improved visibility. Candles were spiked on a cast-iron candle holder with two pins underneath so the candle could be held on the edge of the trawl tub.

Baiting proceeded very rapidly. A normal daylight set was three or three-and-a-half tubs of trawl—some 1,550 to 1,800 or more hooks per two-man dory. The trawl lines were lifted out of the tub and put on the top of the cabin or on upset tubs down in the hold. You took the end of the trawl line on top and stuck the loop through one of the holes in the trawl tub top. This loop would tie the trawl line or ground line to the anchor or to another ground line in the next tub when the gear was set. You then picked up the hook and the coils of trawl line with one hand, and grabbed a piece of chopped bait with the other. You hooked the bait through both skin sides and dropped the coils with the baited hook free of the coil down into the tub. If the trawl line was lifted straight up and then out when setting, you rarely would have a snarl even though the hooks with baits were loose from the ground line.

You then worked your way through the tub, picking up coils, hook, and bait, and with a smooth running motion of your hands you dropped the baited hooks and coils, one after another, into their tub. Two good dorymen could bait 1,200 to 1,500 hooks in an hour and forty five minutes to two hours.

When the gear was baited, you would be ready to go just as the light came into the east. The baited trawl tubs were quickly passed up forward into the vessel's waist between the nested dories. The gear was grouped in the order of setting of the dories. The port dories were numbered with odd numbers, 1, 3, 5, 7, etc., and the starboard dories, 2, 4, 6, 8, etc. The top dories served as the receptacles for the oars and sails of the dories beneath. These were quickly unloaded. The four dorymen in the two top dories

A Doryman's Day

would jump into the dories and begin to ready them, pounding in the dory plugs and setting up their thwarts and kid boards (checkerboards that were set under the second thwart and the stern thwart and held against the dory frames by small cleats). The kid boards formed a pen in the dory's waist and prevented the caught fish from sliding loose and getting underfoot. The four oars were taken from the bottom of the dory and laid ready to use on the thwarts.

The dory's spritsail would be handed in and the trawl tubs, anchors, lines, and buoys would quickly follow and be set into the spaces bounded by the kid boards. The dorymen would already have stowed their water bottle and "bait butt." Some of the water bottles were leather, but most were glass and well covered with sennit or cord wrappings to serve as a buffer against breaking. Most of these water bottles held a maximum of a quart to two quarts. The "bait butt" was a box made of wood or leather that held a dory compass, spare nippers, sometimes some pemmican or hardtack, and sometimes some tobacco (chew or some makings). If smoking tobacco was carried, there was usually a small metal container of "waterproof matches" in the "bait butt." This was also your survival kit if you were lost or went astray. The dories also carried a cone-shaped galvanized foghorn. The schooner carried a large foghorn operated with a pump handle. In fog with dories out, this horn was blown constantly to apprise the dories of the vessel's location. The vessel also carried a small cannon that was used when dories were seriously astray and fog was very thick. In thick fog the directions and intensity or closeness of sound were deceptive. Going astray in a thick fog or winter snow squall was a constant fear shared by all, and particularly by the skipper.

With their gear onboard, the top dories would be hoisted outboard and held in the slings ready to go. The bowman would have passed the painter up to a remaining crewman on deck who rove it up and around the after foremast shroud and then back to the seated bow doryman who held it and braced himself for

FISHERMEN WORKING on their trawl lines aboard a
schooner at Boston, c. 1920.

Sidney M. Chase photograph, Maine Maritime Museum

A Doryman's Day

FISHERMEN WORKING on their trawl lines on a schooner at Boston, c. 1920. The bundles of line are piled atop the cabin, with the empty tubs stacked on the deck next to the fishermen.

Sidney M. Chase photograph, Maine Maritime Museum

the set. The stern doryman would be braced aft to let go the stern hook and then would be ready to begin setting the trawl gear as soon as the dory was dropped.

The skipper would blow the whistle and the port dory would immediately throw overboard its high-flier buoy and as the vessel steamed along at speeds of from 5–7 knots, the buoy line would run out. When approximately 10 fathom of buoy line remained, the stern doryman would lift up the remaining coils of buoy line, the anchor, and the first few coils of baited trawl line and throw them outboard. The dory would immediately be lowered to the water with the stern first, and the stern man would let go of the dory tackle hook. He would yell "away" or "she's clear," or some such thing and immediately grab an oar to use as a sweep to push the dory away from the schooner. By this time the forward dory tackle hook would have been slipped, and the bow doryman would be holding the dory to the vessel with the painter. Upon hearing that "she's clear," he would drop the painter that he had been holding and the dory would shear away from the schooner. The starboard dory would then set its buoy as soon as the port dory was gone or on the skipper's command. As dories were set, the next dory in the nest was rigged and swung outboard. Dories were set port and starboard, port and starboard, until all were gone.

After clearing the vessel the bowman in each dory would coil the bow painter, then immediately unship his oars and start to row to leeward, or if the wind was right, he would set the spritsail and the dory would sail off to leeward, setting trawl as she went.

The stern man would face forward and insert a "lifter," a short, 18- to 20-inch round hardwood stick, under one or two gangings and coils in the tub. He would lift them up and out with a circular throwing motion, and then lift another few coils and gangings. His heaving hand moved in an easy circular motion about one foot in diameter. The trawl line was set with little slack. If necessary the man setting would belay the trawl line to get slack out of the trawl line or if it was too tight, the doryman

SCHOONER SETTING A DORY.

Giles M. S. Tod photograph, not dated, Maine Maritime Museum

THE STERN OF THE MARJORIE PARKER. Undated photograph.
Courtesy of Gordon W. Thomas Collection,
Cape Ann Historical Museum, Gloucester, Massachusetts

A Doryman's Day

THE SCHOONER MARJORIE PARKER, which Barry Fisher fished
aboard in 1946. Undated photograph.

Courtesy of Peabody Essex Museum, Salem, Massachusetts

would lay on his oars or ease the spritsail sheet to slow down and gain slack while his dorymate continued to set trawl.

As the top dories were dropped and set their trawls downwind, the vessel would continue her course over the grounds, running across the wind. If it was possible to set and haul close to slack tide, this was preferable. The distance between the dories was determined largely by how much ground the skipper wanted to cover on a set. Sometimes dories would be very close — fifty to sixty yards apart. Other times you might be a couple of hundred yards apart. On rare instances, on narrow tongues of ground, half the dories would be set up on the top of the ground and the remaining half would be set below them.

As soon as the schooner had set all of the dories, she would generally come about, shut down the engine, and jog back and forth under sail power waiting for the dories to finish. Both vessels I was in, the MARJORIE PARKER and the ROBERTSON II, had a gaff and boom foresail, a big clubbed fore-staysail, and a "leg of mutton" riding sail on the mainmast.

As one tub was set, the top line from the next tub would be tied onto the end of the preceding tub until all gear was set. At the end of the last line in the last tub, another buoy line equivalent in length to the weather or upwind buoy line, was bent onto the end of the trawl's second anchor and thrown overboard, anchoring the gear on bottom. The buoy line was run out and tied to a buoy similar to the weather buoy but without a high flier. The buoy was tied on and thrown overboard to serve as the leeward mark of the trawl line.

The dories would then row or sail downwind to the schooner and be picked up, their tubs and gear passed quickly aboard, the thwarts and kid boards broken down, and the dories hoisted aboard and nested one inside the other.

At this point it was usually just after sunrise, and the cook would have breakfast on. He would yell, "Breakfast" or ring a bell. The whole crew could not eat at the table at once, so one doryman in every pair would go to breakfast at the "Skipper's

Table" while his dorymate remained on deck and began to get bait out and ready the spare tubs of trawl for the day's second set while his dorymate ate.

I would not dare now to count the calories that we consumed on those dory vessels. The meals were gargantuan, and former Surgeon General Koop or Richard Simmons would probably have keelhauled all of us for the grub we put away, but we needed the food. Food was oftentimes a substitute for sleep.

Breakfast normally consisted of some kind of fruit and porridge (oatmeal, cream of wheat, or a porridge of hardtack, milk, butter, and brown sugar). Eggs, potatoes, usually two breakfast meats or a breakfast meat and fish, or leftovers such as salt codfish hash, finnan haddie, or "brews" (salt cod, potatoes, butter, onions, milk, and hardtack cooked together) constituted the second course. There was also bread and toast, sometimes pancakes or French toast, and muffins which were called "dory plugs" (as they bore a physical resemblance to the real dory plugs), doughnuts, fried bread, and some pie or cake leftover from the day before. It was also common to see raisins, currants, or dried prunes in bowls on the table.

You ate as much as you wanted, as fast as you could, and then dumped the slops from your plate, rinsed your mug, plate, and utensils in a bath of fresh water on one side of the stove, and then went on deck. The cook would wash the dishes and again adroitly set the table, often with the engineer's help. (So long as no black greasy fingerprints were inscribed on the inside of the plate or mug by the engineer, no one squawked.) You relieved your dorymate on deck, and he would go down and eat at the mate's table. You would continue the baiting work your dorymate had started.

By this time the skipper would probably have started jogging the vessel up slowly to weather in preparation for dropping you off to haul on the first set. Your dorymate would have eaten by now and would be back up on deck ready to go. Also by this time we generally had at least one tub of trawl baited for the second set. We continued to bait spare gear for the second set until the skipper ordered us into the dories.

The vessel would line up just to windward of the leeward buoys and you would jump into your dory and begin to rig it just as you had when dropped earlier. Dory plugs were pounded in, spritsails, oars, bait butts, water jugs, foghorn, etc., were quickly passed aboard. The empty trawl tubs into which you would coil your gear were passed into the dory's waist.

The dories were swung out and dropped, generally 70 or 80 yards upwind of the lee buoy so you could get everything rigged while you were drifting down on your buoy. The buoy would be gaffed and brought aboard, the buoy line being passed into the sheave of the dory roller (a deeply grooved, hardwood roller wheel). The roller was set into the dory's starboard cap-rail, well forward.

Both men would stand up with the forward man hauling as fast as he could and the after man coiling the buoy line onto a dory thwart until the anchor was hove to the roller and then the line, anchor, and trawl line would be separated and the coiled buoy line tied up and stowed. The buoy, buoy line, and anchor were stowed in the stern. The loop end of the trawl line would be stuck through one of the holes at the top rim of the trawl tub, and the bowman would commence to haul, flipping baits off any empty hooks as they came. When he came to a hook with a fish, he would reach down with his right hand, grab the ganging, swing the fish aboard and back over his right hip, and snap and shake the ganging so as to snap the fish loose.

Usually you could unhook nine out of ten haddock this way and most small codfish. If the fish had swallowed the hook or it was caught through hard tissue, you would take a small hand gaff, run the gaff down the ganging, lift the gaff and fish up in the air, put the ganging and ground line down in your other hand, and shake the gaff. This would shake the fish free. Big cod and halibut or large pollock would be gaffed and brought in, since their weight or liveliness was too much for the gangings.

A Doryman's Day

As the bowman hauled, he would throw the retrieved line out and into the water on the weather or windward side of the dory, and his dorymate, who would be coiling, would allow a 10- to 20-foot loop of trawl line to trail off into the water to weather. He would then begin to coil as has been described before, placing the coils of ground line and the ganging with hook placed on top of the coils into the trawl tub. To try and pass the trawl line straight aft through the dory would cause too many snags.

The bowman would continue to pull, usually in very short bights of no more than 18 to 20 inches. Your knees would be braced against the fore thwart and you would lean back slightly against the weight of the ground line. If you needed to stop, to bring in a fish, to clear a skate or a dogfish from the hook, you would bend over and do it, but you would always hold the ground line with your left hand belayed against your left hip or by your knee against the bow thwart. Hauling was arduous work, particularly if you were facing a strong tide, or a wind and sea.

The dory schooners fished surprisingly tough weather. We would fish in wind conditions of 15 to 20 miles per hour and more, with seas up to 8 or 9 feet. Hauling trawl against such conditions, however, would soon exhaust you. You and your dorymate would change places, he would haul and you would coil. You would continue through the gear, slatting off the fish, and coiling the gear down into the empty tubs.

If the fishing was heavy, you would probably change places every five or six lines, 260 to 320 hooks. The hard weather did not bother us too much beyond the early exhaustion that could set in under such conditions. Naturally everybody preferred flat, calm, clear weather, but if you had that all the time, every farmer, goat roper, and hog jockey in the country would be fishing.

A word now should be said about trawl maintenance. Most repairs to the trawls were done while you were fishing. Each dory had hook sets as part of the personal equipment owned by the dorymen. These were small jigs of nails in a hardwood block in a pattern that resembled a hook set in wood with a carved ridge

SCHOONER ROBERTSON II hoisting in dories. The short rig and the exhaust stack for the engine can be clearly seen. The author fished from this schooner in 1947. Undated photograph.

Courtesy of the Fisheries Museum of the Atlantic Collection, Lunenburg, Nova Scotia

ROBERTSON II just before launching, probably when new in 1940.

Courtesy of Maritime Museum of the Atlantic, Halifax, Nova Scotia

shaped like a hook. If you had a straightened hook, you quickly fitted this into the jig by dropping it down over the nails, pulling on the shank of the hook, and reforming the hook to its original shape. If a hook was dull a new one was slipped on. If a ganging was frayed or didn't look right, you had spare gangings with hooks on them looped around the riser board in the stern of the dory. You quickly bent on a new ganging and hook and kept on coiling. If the ground line was frayed in a spot, you would quickly cut it and tie the two ends of now sound groundline together with a fisherman's knot.

A coiler had time for these repairs. He could always coil slack trawl faster than the bowman could pull the weight of the trawl line and slat fish. The man in the bow would always use a swell or chop to help him. When the dory rose, the ground line was held fast across his left hip. When the dory fell off a chop or swell, you hauled as fast as possible.

On good fishing, the dories would rapidly begin to fill. In good weather dories could carry 1,800 pounds of fish and sometimes more. They would look perilously low, but they were in no danger. Remember the lapstrake planking and the tremendous sheer and flare the dories had. In bad weather we never put much more than 1,200 or 1,300 pounds' weight in them. When your gear was hauled, you rowed or sailed down to the vessel to unload or "lighten."

In the event that you had really heavy fishing, you would rapidly fill the dory to capacity. You would then have to lighten or bring your fish to the vessel. The trawl line was untied at a line junction (remember there were ten lines to a tub). The lee buoy in the dory was tied onto the trawl line remaining in the water. The buoy was dropped overboard and then you would row or sail toward the vessel. When you approached the vessel, the bow painter would be made fast and the skipper or the engineer would hold the stern off with a boathook. You would then begin to pitch the fish aboard the vessel into deck pens alongside the cabin.

The vessel continued to lay as the other dories came down to lighten. Generally catches were about equal between the dories. Only rarely would you see some dories get conspicuously more than the others.

After you lightened, you immediately rowed back up to your end buoy, where you had left off, picked up the buoy, and commenced hauling and coiling. To lighten once in three tubs of trawl was fairly common. Usually you got most of your trip in two or three sets. You "hunted" for fish until you hit them. I've seen some sets where we physically could not contain all of the fish caught in the dories, and the schooner's deck was filled from transom to bow. We had to slat fish off the gear because decks, dories, and holds were full. That was great fun and cause for elation, but Lord, God, it made for extra work.

Keep in mind that if a ten-dory vessel just filled her dories on a good early set, that was 18,000 to 20,000 pounds for the set. And if you got another set in that day with an equivalent or a slightly lower amount of fish, it would only take you three or four days to fill the vessel, and sometimes that day there would be a third set of a tub and a half to two tubs.

As soon as you had all of your gear aboard and coiled in the tubs, you retrieved the high-flier buoy line, stowed it up, and either unshipped oars and rowed for the vessel, or if you had the right kind of wind and enough of it, you rigged the spritsail and sailed down. Dories were easier to row or sail when full. They were high sided and awkward when light. On a fine day with good fishing and enough wind to make it lively, this passage was probably one of the doryman's greatest delights. The world was a grand place then—you got a good rest sailing down and time to talk to your dorymate. Remember that by this time you would have been up and working hard without a break except for breakfast for some six hours, and the long part of the day was still in front of you.

The dories were boarded again and by this time the skipper and the engineer had set up the checkerboards around the cabin and after part of the vessel, which made pens on deck to hold the fish. They also had rolled into position the big 500-pound-capacity wooden tubs on each side aft of the mainmast, and these were then filled with water into which the ripped and gutted fish would be thrown and washed.

The "hold men" came aboard and immediately went down into the hold through the main hatch and rigged wooden chutes down which the dressed fish would slide. They also began to chop up ice to mix in with the fish, which would be stowed neatly in the pens, head to tail, tail to head, in rows.

By this time the rippers and gutters were already at work. All "shack" fish and halibut were bled, ripped, and gutted. From April to November, the fish were also gilled. The rippers would move through the fish, slicing the belly cavity open and dropping the fish into gutting checkers where the gutters picked them up, tore out the guts, and dropped the entrails into a checker with water in it so that the livers would float free and could be barreled for sale. Remember those were the days of cod-liver oil, before Merck, Johnson & Johnson, and others had synthesized everything. We would get ten to twelve barrels of livers per trip. This money was split equally amongst the crew; the vessel did not get a share.

The dressed fish were thrown into a washtub, stirred around to wash them thoroughly, and then passed down via wooden chutes into the hold where they were carefully stowed and iced. The fish were culled for stowage, not only by species, but also by size. There was haddock and haddock scrod, or small haddock, of which we caught very little as the hook was a natural conservation device. Cod was segregated by size in the pens into whale, large, markets, and scrod. Halibut was carefully dressed and iced down, white belly up, with the kidney blood along the backbone, gills, and entrails removed.

Dory schooners always received a premium for their fish. The neat stowage of fish head to tail and tail to head across the run of the pen was one reason. The fish also had good muscle fiber, as they had not been crushed like fish in a dragger's cod end. They also were handled better. The pews or forks that we used had a single or at most a double tine, and you tried always to pew fish in the head, not through the body. Finally, the pens on the schooner were less massive and the fish were not crushed as badly in the hold as they were on draggers. In Canada in 1947 no pews were allowed; all fish were handled by hand.

Because of the large number of men, fish was very rapidly dressed and stowed on dory schooners. The MARJORIE PARKER carried nine dories, the ROBERTSON II carried twelve. On the PARKER we could board, dress, and stow upwards of 20,000–25,000 pounds in an hour and a half. On the ROBERTSON II, we could handle close to 40,000 pounds per hour or better if the fish were of a decent size. All hands except the cook worked at dressing and stowing. The skipper and engineer generally pewed fish into the hold.

While the last of the fish were being cleaned up, a couple of the hold men would begin passing up buckets of bait again for continued baiting of the trawl gear for the second set. Usually the skipper and the engineer would begin to wash the boat down as the fish dressing was cleaned up. The dorymen would begin to bait as rapidly as possible. Remember that we had already baited some gear, a tub or a tub and a half per dory, before being dropped off to haul on the first set.

At about this time, sometime between 9:30 and 10:15 in the morning, the cook would yell, "DINNER!" and dinner it was! A normal dinner had a thick and nourishing soup (we were not consommé connoisseurs) with lots of meat, vegetables, rice, noodles, or fish in it; a "big meat," which was a roast of some sort, or roast chicken, or a salted or smoked meat; a "small meat," which means something that was fried, like small steaks or pork chops, liver, fried chicken, sometimes hamburger, etc.; potatoes; two or three vegetables; fresh bread and sometimes rolls; a wet dessert, like a pudding; and a dry dessert of pie or cake. There was also odd stuff on the table like olives, pickles, cans of sardines, cheese, etc.

When I first went aboard dory schooners as a young seventeen-year-old—six-foot-three long, big mouth, and all appetite between my toenails and my eyebrows—I thought I'd died and gone to heaven when I saw all that grub.

The cooks were good. They were great bakers (and more about that later). Most of them could butcher. They practiced incredible economy of motion in providing so much food for big crews. Neither they nor their galleys would have passed state food and health inspections, but none of us ever died from botulism or salmonella or food poisoning or what have you, although today all restaurants are thoroughly inspected by the authorities and people do die because of these maladies.

You'll note that I didn't mention salads. In that era almost all the dorymen were Nova Scotians or Newfoundlanders who had been brought up to eat root vegetables; green and leafy vegetables were entirely foreign to them and somewhat suspect because they sometimes had bugs in them. A potato or a turnip, if it had a bug, he was boiled into jelly and hence the tuber was safe. Lettuce was not. Tomatoes were liked and were eaten with butter or mayonnaise.

We also used very little fresh milk. Evaporated milk was preferred for porridge, pudding, or for tea and coffee. We had a great deal of salt and smoked food. Again this was a product of the times and places from which the dorymen came. Smoked shoulder, corned beef, salt horse, salt brisket, salted spare ribs, and yes, even junks of salt pork fried in slices, bacon, and lots of sausage. We ate salt codfish, salt mackerel, salt herring, corned hake, kippers, and salted cod tongues and cheeks.

The first table would have gone down at the cook's call to dinner, eaten, and gone back on deck. Your dorymate on the mate's table would have gone below to eat. Even though we on the first table helped the cook by swilling out our plates, mugs, and flatware, it was still quite a trick for the old boy to wash and rinse them, get them back on the table, and replenish all the plates, bowls, and servers with fresh grub for the second table. He usually managed to do this in no more than ten to fifteen minutes.

The baiting of the trawls would continue for the second set. The second set was usually anywhere from two to three tubs of trawl depending on the fishing and how much fish the vessel had already caught.

All during this time the skipper would have been maneuvering the vessel into the position he wanted for the second set. At his signal the dories were readied again and the first two slung outboard, and the second set would begin. We would set the gear as previously described and come back to the vessel. In calm weather sometimes not all of the dories were picked up. Three or four or more on each side of the stern would be tied off with the first dory's painter made fast to the stern bits and the other dories tied bow painter to the stern becket of the dory in front of them in a line. Some dories on a larger vessel like the ROBERTSON II would be boarded and nested.

The gear would generally be left to soak for one and a half to two hours. This time period was used as a catch-up time for most of the dorymen. We would tie up some new trawl lines, make new gangings, overhaul anchor lines, etc. Today's fishermen cannot realize how much work there was in the old days trying to keep up with fishing gear that was made of natural fibers such as cotton, linen, Manila hemp, etc. The average ganging would only last for a few sets. The ground lines were probably good for no more than a month. The buoy lines, maybe six weeks. In addition to being short-lived, the strength of the natural fibers when they were new was on an order of magnitude of some five to ten times or more weaker than today's artificial fibers of the same size. To all of these troubles, you would have to add rot of the gear lying wet in the trawl tubs from the time the vessel left the grounds to go in, through her shore time, and back out again. And if you ran into dogfish, they would fray the gear so badly that you would have to make up complete replacement gear.

Dogfish-laden trawl lines were killers to haul, agony to slat, usually slowed you down, and the set would take three to four hours to complete.

Remember, too, that almost everything we used was made of wood and this wood—in the form of dories, thwarts, kid boards, oars, tubs, etc.—took a very heavy beating. Dories, gear, and fishing gear was thrown around at high speed and without too much thought for easy landings. Dory and dory gear repair was a constant.

We also used this time to have a mug-up, a short gam with shipmates or your dorymate, and a smoke or two. It would now be mid afternoon, and the skipper would tell us to get ready again. The vessel was put into position, the dories set out just to windward of the leeward buoys again, and we would lay on to haul. The second set followed the pattern of the first set. The gear was hauled and coiled, the fish boarded in the waist of the dory, the dory transported the fish to the vessel, and then dories were boarded and fish was dressed similar to the morning set.

A decision would be made while the last of the fish was being dressed and put down whether or not we would make a third set for the day. If we only needed 10,000–15,000 pounds to fill her, or if we needed another 10,000–15,000 pounds to put us comfortably over the one-third full or the two-thirds full mark, we would probably make another set, usually two or two and a half tubs per dory.

If the skipper felt that we didn't need this extra fish, we would be done for the day, except for a cleanup and scrubdown of the vessel, and making up new gear if that was needed. By this time it was usually 5:00 or 6:00 PM and we had put in a fourteen-hour day. If we did need another set, the gear would be baited, loaded into the dories and readied, and we would come aboard for supper.

Supper was about the same as dinner. The same soup, a couple of meats or a meat and a fish entrée, potatoes, two or three vegetables, bread pudding, fruit, pie, or cake, cheese, etc. We only had two pieces of crockery with which to eat our meals—a sturdy mug and a thick shallow soup plate made of industrial or "diner"-grade china. Rarely would this plate ever touch the table when eating soup. It was held in your hand to constantly balance against the vessel's roll. You ate soup first—with a very big soup spoon; you most likely ate bread or hardtack with it, and if you were fastidious, you would wipe up the last drops of soup with a crust of bread. I was never fastidious, the soup—no matter what it was—always mixed well with the next course for me. The same went for your plate after you had consumed the entrées and accompaniments—you wiped out the remnants with a crust of bread and then ate your dessert. Oftentimes people would lick out the remnants of the dessert from the plate (you see, we didn't have our mothers there to tell us not to).

If we were not going to set again, the skipper's table would gather on deck or go aft by the cabin, and we'd all stand around with our hands in our pockets, smoking pipes or cigarettes, or chewing. We would commence to talk about everything: some damned trip made thirty-eight or forty-five years ago, parties, booze, women, hunting, sports, stupid-fishermen stories, gossip, scandalous current events, and the relative success of the Boston Red Sox. Usually, as you all know, if it were late in the baseball season, there was no relative success associated with the Red Sox—there was only grim reality. But in 1946 when I was on the PARKER, the Red Sox went to the World Series. Those were good, good times.

We enjoyed each other very much as shipmates and even though the old fellows crabbed and groused all the time, they were pretty happy, too. Between you and your dorymate, there had to be a very special relationship. You had to like each other very much. You had to be willing to give the best that was in you to work with your dorymate. The word dorymate, when I was a boy in Gloucester, was the highest word of respect and affection that one man could use for another.

You knew who you were, you knew the caliber of your

shipmates, and you were doing skilled work and took pride in it. You had your health (at least I did), you ate well, and you slept sound. It is easy now, over five decades later, to be nostalgic or overly sentimental, but those men in those two vessels were the finest I have ever known. They were tough and yet gentle. They were polite and considerate in their behavior, and yet rowdy in their humor. They would tease you one minute (especially me, a seventeen-year-old) and praise you the next. They were physically tough and courageous. Most were generous to a fault. They were, without a doubt, the best small-boat seamen I have ever seen, and, along with the Portuguese dorymen, probably the best the world has ever seen.

The cook meantime would be below deck getting his baking going for the next morning. He would bake bread and some pastry one day, and cake, pies, crullers, turnovers, muffins, or what have you the next. The bread would be started, kneaded, and left to rise with a damp towel covering it. Sometimes he made enough dough to fry some the next morning as fried bread dough. If he were baking his sweet stuff, the pastry would be rolled out, the cake dough mixed, the puddings made and put into the ice box. The pie tins and cake pans would be filled, covered by a damp towel, and waiting on the sideboards, ready to go into the oven as soon as he got up in the morning. The coal fire would be banked for the night. In the early morning the watch made up his fire for him and got the stove hot. They would also knead his bread again during the night.

The amount of baked goods consumed was considerable. Cooks used to figure one-half of a loaf of bread per day, per man. They figured a third of a pie, a third of a cake, and six or seven other pieces of pastry per day, per man. They reckoned that each man would probably eat a good three or four cups of pudding per day.

The cook would be done with his day at 9:00 PM or so; whether you had continued to fish or had quit after your third set at 10:00 at night, he was done. He might have gotten a twenty-minute or half-hour nap sometime between lunch and the conclusion of the second set. More often than not, he lived on four or five hours' sleep a day, and he cooked from the time the vessel left, through the trip, until she was tied up again, and then he usually had to have plenty of pie and cakes to go with tea and coffee for mug-ups for the crew while we took the fish out, and for such visitors who would come aboard the vessel for a visit and a gam.

If we had made a third set, we would be dropped on to haul after supper. We would have set before supper. In the summertime we would have sufficient light to complete the set, but not in the winter. In the wintertime we carried crude kerosene lanterns in the dory for night work. They were cans with a cover 12 to 14 inches in diameter. They were made of galvanized sheet, some 8 to 10 inches high. A metal wick stand and a cloth wick extended up from the top of this torch pan some 8 inches. The wick stand had a cover which was removed and the lamp wick lit when needed. They were smelly, they were smoky, and they threw indifferent light, but you could get by with them.

By the time we were back from the third set, it was usually 9:00 PM and we had fish to dress and put down and the vessel to clean up. If she was full, we'd scrub her off extra well with salt and water and crude boat soap. The trawl tubs would be scrubbed and washed and everything sloshed down as best as we could make it. The gear was secured and lashed down as were the dories in their cradles.

If you had enough fish to go home, the watches would be immediately set with each dory providing a man at the wheel and a man on lookout at the bow. In rough weather the lookout generally was in the pilothouse on the stern, but always in rough weather there was more than one dory crew up. Sometimes the watches were doubled or tripled, as in the case of thick fog.

If the vessel was not full and you were remaining for more days of fishing, the night would be split into watches, with each pair of dorymen standing one watch. The vessel would be pumped

UNLOADING FISH from a schooner at Boston, c. 1920.

Sidney M. Chase photograph, Maine Maritime Museum

A Doryman's Day

out at the end of every watch by hand pumps with brakes and the next watch called.

The average time spent on a trip was partly dependent upon the time of the year. Trips averaged from four to six days in summer, and six to nine or ten days in winter. In the late spring, summer, and fall we fished the channel between George's Bank and Cape Cod, or the Northern Edge of George's Bank in the MARJORIE PARKER. In the wintertime we would run across to western Nova Scotia and take bait in Yarmouth, Shelburne, or Lockeport. We would watch the weather and come out and fish LeHavre Bank or Roseway Bank or sometimes Brown's Bank. If a bad breeze came up, you could get into a Nova Scotia port from those areas in five or six hours.

A great many of the crews came from that part of the world or had been shipmates or dorymates with men who lived in those towns, so there were always visitors in the galley and the cooks were always dishing out grub to the visitors and to us. There were a lot of good cribbage games, checkers, red dog, and whist. There were always stories, too, and sometimes poems in the epic style that the dorymen liked.

On board the ROBERTSON, of course, Roseway and LeHavre were in our front yard. If it looked as if there were going to be a couple of good days of weather, the skipper called us, and we went down to the cold-storage room in the fish plant, got our bait, and would bait at least five tubs per dory. We'd fish as long as the weather would allow, or until we filled her.

When I was in the ROBERTSON II, winter storms gave me a great deal of time to spend with a girlfriend I had in Shelburne. After leaving the MARJORIE PARKER I spent the summer in the schooner JORGINA SILVEIRA swordfishing out of Gloucester. We always visited back and forth in the evening in the swordfish fleet on these fishing grounds, and I knew most of the gang on both the ROBERTSON and the ROBERTSON II. On our third trip of the season, a swordfish had punched the dory as I was hauling him and his sword laid open my leg which rapidly became infected. I was landed in Shelburne and treated in the Shelburne hospital. While there, I met a very lovely girl and we became very close. I had to go home and finish the season, but while out on our last trip, I was asked by the skipper of the ROBERTSON II, who was a friend of my girl's father, if I would like to come down and go dorymates in the fall with Angus MacAskell, whom I knew quite well. I agreed. When the season was over, I took the ferry to Yarmouth, was met by my young friends, and I went fishing. No Immigration, no Customs, no nothing.

Later, the local "Mounty" (Royal Canadian Mounted Police), who was a great friend of my girl's dad, was asked by a visiting Immigration officer who knew I was going with Harley's daughter, "Is that young Yank, the one going with Harley's girl, is he in the country legal?"

The Mounty is reputed to have looked at him and said, "You're right, me son, he is going with Harley's daughter, and they get along the finest kind. He is on the ROBERTSON II and Perc, the skipper, tells me he's right spry and lively. He's a good hand. So you see, me son, he's family. Do you get my drift? He's family."

When I think now of the closeness of community that we had then amongst vessels and men and places, it makes me glad I knew those times. The world was much simpler. Of course, in many respects the good old days were not so good. I can remember teeth being pulled in a schooner's cabin with a pair of pliers, broken limbs splinted and the man put in the bunk while the vessel finished the trip, sicknesses that couldn't be treated, etc.

But we all knew who we were and we lived by fairly simple rules. Captain Frank Hynes of the schooner MARJORIE PARKER was something of an oral poet, and he had a way with words. During my time on the vessel he said at one time or another words to me which I put together in the summer of 1994 and called "A Doryman's Legacy." They sum up pretty well for me the quality of the company I kept then and the rules by which I've since tried to live.

I was on wheel watch one night when the captain came up

on deck from the cabin. He checked the compass and said, "Young fellah, mind the course, steady as she goes, steer small."

Then after a pause he said, "Face storms and the shoals of adversity square on. Remember, one hand for the vessel first, always first, and then one hand for yourself.

"When, as they sometimes will, danger and death loom over the horizon and stand down upon you, don't panic. Meet them with your dorymate and shipmates, stand well braced and fend them off.

"Go joyously into the dory; whatever job of work there be, give it the finest and the best that is in you. Be good to your dorymate and your shipmates. Speak no ill of them.

"If you go aground, work yourself off. Cast off all self-pity and beat to windward again and again and again, so that in the fullness of your years, you can come about and run downwind free and easy with the tide.

"If life gives you more baitings than most, share some of these extra rations with your dorymate and shipmates and them who have not been so lucky as you.

"Remember, Life is a grand dance—pay the Old Fiddler as you enjoy it and find a good partner to dance with and to love. Do you understand, young fellah? Do you get my drift?"

Mysterious Ways of the LORD

or
How Captain Jack Brant of the
Swordfishing Schooner LORNA B
Found God in a Split Second
and Then Achieved Salvation on the
Northern Edge of George's Bank

The year 1948 wasn't much of a swordfish year for the Gloucester swordfishing fleet.

Fish had been scarce and spotty no matter where the fleet went. The best trips had only been about seventy-five fish or so, and on the third trip of the season, which covered the month of September, none of the vessels had done better than sixty-five fish; most had less than fifty fish.

The whole fleet was ready to hang it up and convert the vessels back to dragging for redfish, with but one exception.

The owner of the schooner LORNA B, a smallish schooner some 65 feet in length, wanted to find someone to take the LORNA B out for one more trip, even though it was now the first part of October. After the autumnal equinox, the twenty-second of September, swordfish had a habit of being real "squitzy," really on the prod, and ready to desert George's Bank and go on off into the warmer waters of the Gulf Stream.

The vessel's owner needed a new pair of winches before the vessel could go back to dragging, and he didn't have the "scratch." His hope was that the boat could catch enough swordfish to let him make a down payment on the winches; otherwise he was sunk, since he couldn't get credit to pay for the winches.

The skipper and crew that had been in the vessel all season swordfishing wanted no part of another trip. The LORNA B had not done as well as the fleet average, and they were more than ready to get back to the serious business of making a living at dragging.

But for a great many men in Gloucester, swordfishing was a "fun" fishery. It was for people who had an itch for sailing in the schooners, spending their days aloft on the fore topmast looking hard for the fins of the swordfish, and then running the vessel down and harpooning the unsuspecting fish. The 100-fathom-long warp (line) would go from the dart of the harpooner's pole stuck into the fish up to a brightly colored buoy on the other end. A dory would be immediately set to pick up the buoy, fight the fish by recovering line, and then finally lance him and strap his tail for delivery from the dory to the schooner.

There, in a couple of mouthfuls, I've described what gave lots of men in Gloucester and Boston "the wants" to go swordfishing every summer. Beyond that, there were good times. In the evening when the fleet shut down men from the various vessels would row back and forth to visit, as did some skippers. There would be tall tales—known as "big lies"—and common everyday lies about fishing, where so-and-so had gotten to, announcements of changes in family during the past year, etc. There were also jokes of every kind, and finally, tales of strength and skill and heroic efforts. You could always tell when one of the incredible tales started. Invariably it began with the words, "This is no B.S., it's the clear truth, me sons." The clear truth was that you would be listening to a whopper.

These visits were also accompanied with "mug-ups" of good things to eat, like pies, cakes, and snacks laid on by the vessel's cook. In the swordfish fleet there were numerous fellows who could scratch a good tune out of a fiddle or play the squeezebox (concertina) or tickle a tune out of a banjo. A lot of us could play the bones—two tablespoons clacking together to provide rhythm for the music—so we sometimes had music and a good sing.

Beyond that, the American boats all engaged in a clandestine trade with the vessels from Nova Scotia. You see, the fish buyers in Nova Scotia would not pay a decent price for swordfish livers, so the Canadian boats would give the livers to us to bring in and sell in Boston. Since tobacco was very dear in Canada, we would bring out cases of cigarettes and pipe tobacco and plenty of chewing tobacco with the money earned from the Canadian swordfish livers. The Canadians would always pay us off in booze, which they purchased out of bond at very low prices. A five-gallon keg of Demerara rum, 151 proof, cost about twenty bucks. You could get French brandy for two dollars a bottle, and Scotch for a dollar and a half.

A Doryman's Day

An added bonus was that swordfishing allowed the crew a good night's sleep. You started up right after sunup, and you shut down at sundown. With seven men aboard the average schooner to stand a short watch, everyone got a lot more sleep than you ever would have had dory fishing or dragging. If the weather was snotty and it was too rough to fish, you could get even more sleep.

The owner of the LORNA B wasn't having too much luck getting a skipper to try another trip in October. Everybody had had enough for one year and didn't think much of the prospects of finding a trip that late in the season. Vessels had come in from fishing in October in years past, but nobody had started out on a trip in October.

After a few days, an old Newfoundlander and swordfish skipper named Jack Brant told the owner he had heard he was looking for a skipper and that he, Jack, was willing to take the vessel for one more trip. The owner agreed and Captain Brant took to the business of finding a crew.

He didn't have to worry about the engineer because engineers in those days were more or less tied to the vessel by reason of extra payments or wages beyond the crew share. The owners did this to ensure the machinery would be taken care of. The engineer was a taciturn man who had retired from the navy as a chief "motor mac" (chief machinist mate). He had come from Missouri and when he had enlisted in the navy he swore that there were two things he would never tolerate again in his life: eating dust and spending ten or twelve hours a day looking at the ass of a mule while piloting a plow. It was natural that he gravitated to Gloucester and liked fishing fairly well.

The first person Jack hired was Nathan Foot, one of the finest cooks that ever shook out a tablecloth in Gloucester, Boston, or New Bedford. Nathan was a gourmet chef and a hell of a baker. He was also a very wise old bird and knew quite a bit about first aid. More than that, he was a boyhood chum of Captain Jack Brant. They both came from Bay Saint Margarets in

Newfoundland. They had been shipmates off and on over the years fishing out of Boston. In fact, Nathan rescued Jack from a misery that had plagued him for most of his adult life.

Jack had started off as a young skipper of dory-fishing schooners in Boston but his inability to control his appetite for booze had lost him the credibility and trust that a skipper has to have with his owners. Jack would go on some horrible binges as the years went on. Finally it was Nathan who nursed Jack out of his dependency on alcohol and into lasting sobriety. As luck would have it, and keeping in mind the oft-stated phrase, "There is no one more dogmatic than a reformed drunk," Jack turned his dogmatism toward religion. He blamed God for his having become a drunk. He was notorious for cursing God when things went wrong. By 1948 Captain Jack Brant was a trustworthy skipper. But his alcoholism had long since cost him any chance of making the big time in Boston or Gloucester as a skipper of dory fishermen or trawlers because he was too old by the time he shook alcohol.

I was next in line among those who came around looking for a site (job). I was a kid, I was single, I really didn't care that much about money, and I would, in those days, jump at any opportunity to go swordfishing. I had put in a summer on another schooner, but I was still eager to give it another shot. Captain Jack shipped me, saying he had heard good things about me as a doryman. He wanted me to go first dory.

Then along came Alec MacCauley, an old-timer in his mid sixties, who asked for the striker's berth. Good strikers or harpooners were probably the most important persons on a swordfisherman. Alec was a good one, but he was also a stone-cold drunk. He was sober that day, he had been sober for a week, and the shakes were gone. Jack hired him with a stern admonishment: "God dammit, you keep your face away from John Barleycorn. You come down eight o'clock every morning and check with me, and by the Lord Jesus, we'll keep you busy and straight."

The next guy to show up looking for a site was Willy Stuart. Willy was the most handsome man I have ever seen—tall, with a good slender build, curly blond hair, and eyes as bright as the hue of a nor'wester. He had a constant white-toothed smile on his face and a beautiful mahogany tan. He spoke very little, answering questions with a yes or no, and volunteered few words of his own. But that constant grin and his pleasant manner made him very popular as a shipmate.

Willy's quiet was a result of horrible combat experiences in World War II. A Scotsman hailing from Cape Breton Island, Nova Scotia, Willy had joined a Canadian Scottish Highlander Regiment of Infantry as soon as he came of age. The regiment had gone in on D-Day in Normandy and Willy went through it all and was badly wounded a week before it was over in Germany. He had been on the line almost constantly, his unit had been riddled with casualties, and Willy had been awarded high British and Canadian decorations for gallantry and heroism. When the Germans wounded him they did it so badly that it was as if the edges of his soul were burned and shriveled away, and what was left was deep inside him to be protected by not making close contact with anyone. But Willy was a good swordfisherman, and Jack knew he would be a good shipmate.

The next guys to come down looking for a site were three Portuguese fellows. One of them, Manuel de Pinto, could speak pretty good English and had been an accomplished crewman in whatever fishery he had been in—doryfishing, dragging, or swordfishing. The other two Portuguese, John and Joaquin, spoke almost no English but I knew of them by reputation and told Jack they were good. Jack hired all three. Now we needed only one man, a mastheadman.

We all spent the day going over the vessel's gear and checking the buoy lines, some of which were pretty frayed by that time so we made up some new ones. We refastened and repaired all of the straps on the buoy kegs. The buoy kegs were 100-pound wooden nail kegs, painted in bright colors individual to each vessel so they could be told apart from other vessels' buoy kegs in the water at sea. Our colors were red and white.

Alec the striker honed up all of the swordfish double-barbed darts to get the leading edges razor sharp. He restrapped all of the darts with brand new buoy line, and then carefully sanded with emery cloth the pikes or rods of the harpoon upon which the darts were set.

At day's end, Alec wanted to borrow five or ten bucks from Jack, and Nathan told him no, that if it was supper he was wanting, he and Jack and Alec could go together to the diner and get a good feed. Alec started to protest but Jack shut it right off. "God dammit, a feed you got coming; booze you don't need. If I catch you drinking booze we'll get another striker."

The next morning we came down to the vessel again. Nathan had made a phone call the night before and at about 9:30, Harvey Atwood, a spry little Newfoundlander and a good mastheadman, was standing on the dock.

"Hey, boy," he yelled at Jack. "They tells me you're after needin' a mastheadman. I be your man."

Jack looked up at him and retorted, "I be the one that says whether or not you're me man, bucko. Don't you forget it."

Nathan came running down the deck, and said, "Boys, boys, boys — have you no common sense at all? Each one of you need the other and the pair of you bastards are acting like you're the high and mighty Prince of Wales — the pair of you! Harvey, go get your bag of rags [seabag gear and fishing clothes]. Jack, Harvey has just shipped with us, ain't that right, Jack?"

Neither one said no, so Harvey completed the swordfish crew for the LORNA B. Harvey was a good mastheadman and like most guys of his height — five foot one inch — he had a cocky and scrappy attitude toward the world. Harvey had gained fame by wearing two-inch Adler Elevated Shoes and being proud of it. One time in the Long Bar at the Boston Fish Pier, Harvey had had half a jag on when some big gorilla of a Newfoundlander began to pick on him for his diminutive size. Harvey swung at him but even with the Adler Elevated Shoes, he was too short to connect with the bigger man's jaw. The big fellow gave Harvey a shove and knocked him twenty feet down the bar. He turned away, laughing, but Harvey wasn't all done. He whipped off one of his shoes, jumped up on the guy's back, got a leg lock around his ribs and a half nelson around his windpipe, and proceeded to beat the livin' bejesus out of him with the heel of his Adler Elevated Shoe. The big guy couldn't dislodge him. Finally the boys in the bar broke it up and the bartender stood a free round for all hands. Harvey, not being content, told the big fella if he ever rolled even an eye at him again, that he, Harvey, would put a face on him that a dog wouldn't look at.

Apparently the reason for Harvey's wanting to go swordfishing again was that his wife had gone out and bought some new living-room furniture, thinking that Harvey would have a good trip and that they could afford it. Harvey hadn't had a good last trip swordfishing, and he berated his wife; she, in turn, told him that it was up to him to make the money, that she would spend it. Harvey told her he would fix her wagon. He had heard that Jack Brant was gonna try one more trip swordfishing and that he was gonna go mastheadman and that if he didn't make much money, of which there was a good chance, then the furniture people could come and drag their sticks out of his house and that she, the old lady, could go sit on a packing crate. With that, he took off and came to Gloucester and became our mastheadman.

We now had the crew. The dories (five of them nested in a cradle on the port side) had been looked over. The gear was okay. It was time to get ice, grub, and fuel oil. By this time all of Gloucester knew we were gonna have another go at it. People around the docks went out of their way to tell us what a bunch of damn fools we were; we were gonna get out there and the fish would be gone—or worse, we'd get just a few fish and the fish would go and we'd have to finish the trip with long day after long day looking for fish that had disappeared into the Gulf Stream. Nobody had ever made a trip starting out after the first of October. It got to be hard to take.

Jack gave orders to sail at two o'clock. A lot of my "friends" had told me they would help me get a job dragging later and save me from the "poorhouse." They said they would lend me enough money to buy my fit-out, gloves and reading material, candy and cigarettes, for the first trip that I would make dragging. Everybody was giving us such good advice! Even my dad questioned the wisdom of such a late trip, and he was no fisherman. It was almost as if they all wanted to put a curse on the trip because we had the temerity not only to try it again, sailing far later than anybody had ever done, but we were doing it at the end of a lousy swordfishing year. And then they started in on the boat. The boat wasn't fit. She was too small to be running around that far offshore that late in the season, when sometimes the hurricanes came slamming out of the equatorial zones, turning from the Caribbean Sea and running and billowing up the East Coast and along the continental shelf.

The LORNA B *was* a smallish vessel. Whatever she had done all of her life, she was too small. She had not been a successful dory fisherman because she couldn't carry enough dories and berths for the dorymen and didn't have a big enough fish hold to make it worthwhile. She had been a marginal producer as a redfish dragger. She could only carry about 60,000 pounds of iced fish. She had been reasonably taken care of, but not well taken care of, and she looked it. There were weep holes of rust running down the chainplates to which the shrouds for the vessel's masts were joined. She leaked a little bit more than most vessels did through her shaft log, from which the propeller protruded. Some of her seams were not as tight as they should be. The caulking was old and tired. The decks had to have water or moisture on them frequently to stay tight, and on the forward deck the seams were so dried out that if not kept wet they would leak water down into the galley and the bunks. But the LORNA B's rigging was good and the engine ran well, and the pumps—both engine-driven and manually operated—were in good shape.

We fell away from the dock a few minutes after two. Jack gave the orders to hoist the riding sail on the mainmast, then to set the fore staysail, and finally, to raise that last sail which still linked the vessel to the days when full sail on a Gloucester schooner was the ultimate. We swayed the boom and gaff foresail on her, and sheeted it home. Jack then made a full circle, following the course of the sun clockwise from east to west after we left the dock, which was one of the old superstitions that swordfishermen had. You turned the vessel clockwise the full circle because if you turned the vessel counterclockwise or against the course of the sun, that was tempting fate and going against the natural order of things. As we stood down the harbor Jack gave three long blasts on the vessel's horn. This, too, was tradition for departing swordfishermen, and the three blasts meant, "goodbye boys, good fishing, and God be with you."

It was a busy harbor that afternoon. Not many people yelled a goodbye. No vessels answered our horn with a return blast wishing us luck. A couple of people on the dock made signs indicating we were crazy, and from the deck of one vessel a voice sang out, "What a bunch of crazy misfits in a junkpile of a boat." I and a couple of other guys flipped them the bird back.

We were soon out of the harbor. Jack laid the course off for the Peaked Hill Bar buoy at the northern tip of Cape Cod, and from there on down to the Northern Edge of George's Bank. The weather was good, a light sou'wester blowing, which let the sails give us a little extra speed. We were on a beam reach. It was a good late-summer's afternoon, not early October weather. Around about five Nathan blew the whistle for supper, and he had gotten us a good one. He had made a fish chowder from a couple of haddock that he had bummed off one of the fish plants, pork chops and onions, boiled potatoes, fresh corn on the cob, pickled beets, and a big fruit pudding. I don't know where the hell that man found the time to whip out such a ration of grub. He was a dandy!

We ran smoothly through the night, averaging a good nine knots or more. The sea was easy, the vessel rolling gently with her sails full. I came on watch about ten o'clock. The course was given to me, along with orders to call Jack at four in the morning, to be passed on to the succeeding watches. The course was east southeast and it was an easy course to hold. It was almost as if the vessel knew where she had to go and was making a good passage toward her destination.

Most of the swordfish schooners in that era, if they could, took off their pilothouses so the helm was open. The helmsman sat on the wheelbox with its big multispoked steering wheel of iron with wooden handles. You would move the wheel sometimes with your hands and sometimes with your feet, following a compass that was tucked into a little cubbyhole in the starboard side of the cabin. Just above the compass was fixed a mirror. It was so angled so that it reflected the compass card and the lubber's line down to the head of the skipper's bunk, so that during the night he could, at a glance, tell if you were on course or off without moving from his bunk.

Toward the end of my watch, there was a little bit of a mist that came in, but not thick. You could still see quite a ways off. The mist sent tiny little moving tendrils of white moisture stealing up over the swell of the sails. There was about three-quarters of a moon and the sails shone silver. The light was so great that you could see all of the individual lines lashing the big foresail to the gaff and to the boom. The gaff and the throat halyards, which lifted up and stretched the sail, were shining like so many black-silver rods. There are few sights to equal the sweet seductive swell of a gaff-rigged sail in soft, misty moonlight.

It was a very content and a very happy watch to stand. The vessel felt great. She steered so easily, seeming almost to anticipate the spoke or two of wheel that I gave to hold her on course. We had a good crew. Given any chance at all, we were going to kill some swordfish.

When I was relieved from my watch, I went down to a very easy sleep. I was only twenty at the time, so before turning in, I ate three ears of cold corn, two pork chops, and a dish of fruit pudding. I found some cookies that Nathan had left out. It was a good sleep on a full belly.

I sensed the vessel shutting down about quarter of five in the morning. We had arrived. We were on the Northern Edge of George's Bank. During the day we would work our way down this edge, hugging the 100-fathom (600 feet of depth) curve until we struck fish. Jack had shut her down so that we wouldn't overrun anything; we would spend the entire day working to the east'ard.

When you're looking for swordfish, there are some sea signs of surface activity that give you clues. A profusion of sea birds—gulls and gannets—wheeling restlessly and endlessly in the air is a good sign. That means there's bait around—herring or mackerel or whiting. They may not be on the surface, but they're there. And, if the feed is plentiful, the predators at the top of the pile—the broadbilled swordfish—might probably be there, too. The same with oily slicks on the surface of the ocean. These are more often than not the oil that comes as a result of these bait fish being cut into pieces by the swordfish's long, sharp sword. The oil floats to the surface. You want to look really close, to see if Mother Carey's Chickens—diminutive little white and sooty-colored birds who worry the surface of the water looking for tiny scraps of bait—are around. These birds never touch the water with their bodies; they fly constantly, plucking up tidbits with their extended legs and feet.

You look for tide rips. These are the edges of blocks of water being moved inexorably by the currents. As tides come and go, the currents change. They do it with great pressure, and the surface dances with little waves and chops as the water masses rub and exert friction against each other's edges. When the tide turns slack and the tide rips run heavy, the swordfish often come up along these edges from depths of ten to thirty fathoms or more to actively feed and then lie on top of the water, basking in the sun, somnolent, and very slow in their movements.

By contrast, there are bad signs, such as a lack of life on the sea's surface. Prevalence of sharks is a bad sign. Swordfish prefer the edges of currents or warm-water/cold-water fronts and layers. Sharks sometimes are numerous behind them, and sword-fish can't bask unperturbed on the surface of the water if there are a lot of sharks around. Some sharks, like the blues, are harmless to swordfish. But there are others who sometimes sneak in and bite the tail off a swordfish; then, when the swordfish loses its strength, they will bite off the sword, and then feast. If a swordfish has its wits about it and is alert, no shark stands a chance against that long, slightly curved, sharp sword which can demolish a dory, cut a shark in half, or drive its point through ten to twelve inches or more of oak.

On board the LORNA B we had a good breakfast. Nathan had some fresh doughnuts for us and told us to eat good but not too much or we'd go to sleep aloft on the fore topmast. Soon after breakfast we started up. Jack had taken cross bearings on the radio direction finder which, if you were lucky, might show you where you were within twenty miles. But like all of the other old-timers, he placed far more reliance on a heaving lead and line. We had an electronic fathometer on the boat, which would show our depth, but Jack liked running the lead line. The lead line had a long cylinder of lead weighing approximately four or five pounds, which had at its base a rounded cup. You put butter or winch grease into this cup so that when the lead hit the bottom a sample of the bottom is pressed into the butter or the grease, and from this you could then tell the composition of the bottom from the sediment samples. Was it sand or mud or clay? If it was hard clay or rock, you wouldn't capture anything in the cup. You gauged the depths with the lead line by the markings that were placed at specified intervals on the line, usually with big marks for ten-fathom increments, and a small mark between for five. Anything remaining over that measure was gauged by the lead-man's arms stretched as wide as possible so as to make up a rough fathom.

When the old-timers would look at that deposit from the lead and the depth measured by the line, after a few soundings of the lead line most of them knew pretty well where they were.

The brains of those old-time Gloucester dory-fishing and sword-fishing captains were, in my opinion, the precursor of the modern computers. Those old buggers knew the continental shelves from below Cape Cod to the extremes of the Grand Bank of Newfoundland, and they knew it by dead reckoning and the lead lines. They knew all of the curves and subterranean canyons of the banks. They knew the high spots and the holes. They knew whether the bottom was fair or foul, and whether the bottom was mud or sand, clay or pea gravel. They knew the movements of fish, the myriad species of cod, haddock, redfish, pollock, hake, and the various soles and flounders. They also knew the movements of the swordfish in response to water temperatures, currents, feed, and the seasons of the summer on the various banks like the Canyons to the southwest of George's Bank and the southeast part of George's and the Nor'east Peak and the run over to Brown's Bank with its Peak of Browns and its long sunken forest of wood called the Trees of Browns. They knew LeHavre Bank and Roseway and the run down to Western Bank and Sable Island. They knew them over Banquereau and St. Pierre's Bank and on over Misaine Bank, over the Gully and onto the Grand Bank of Newfoundland, which stretched for scores and scores of miles, known to generations of Gloucester dory fishermen. Grand Bank yielded the biggest swordfish of all, averaging 350 to over 400 pounds dressed. You didn't get many fish down there, but when you got them they were monsters.

But the only chance we had this late in the year was to run out the season on George's Northern Edge and maybe, if the fish then left the grounds, to run eighty or ninety miles off to the southeast part of the bank and hope to make a stand there that would be worthwhile.

Jack gave the orders to start up and go aloft, and he swung the vessel again in a full circle, as we got our "oilskins" (foul-weather gear) on, tied our long-billed swordfish caps on our heads, and stuffed our pockets with toilet paper to wipe eyes that would be burning with strain and the sea glare by day's end. We put on our gloves, swayed up in the riggin', and started aloft to the topmast lookout stations. Harvey the mastheadman was the first to go. Nathan sent him off with a blessing, "Harvey, me son, Harvey me bucko, you're a credit to the island of Newfoundland and you're climbing that f-----g stick like the best monkey that ever lived. Keep your eyes peeled aloft." Harvey looked down and he said, "Ah, Nathan me boy, Nathan me darlin', you're the grandest belly robber that ever run from the rock of Newfoundland. Don't pee in the soup!"

We all managed to get up onto the foretopmast. The foretopmast was 20 feet in length and was tapered from bottom to top, from 8 inches at the butt to 6 inches at the peak. The foretopmast was stepped at the hounds and the foremast spreaders of the foremast peak on top. It was anchored in place by a strong iron linchpin running through spacer blocks made fast to the foremast spreaders and a hole at the butt of the topmast. The mast then went up through a ring of galvanized iron that was fastened to the very top of the foremast. The peak (or the top) of the topmast had a mastheadman's collar fitted snug over the wood. The collar was made of galvanized iron that curved around on each side in a tight semicircle so as to hold the mastheadman in and give him something to which he could cling. This iron collar was heavily padded with strips of burlap and it had slots in the extremities of each collar end into which could be clipped a safety belt, which passed around the mastheadman's back, and a board with lines on it and clips which fastened in place to give him a seat. At his feet there was a board lashed to the topmast upon which he could rest his feet.

The topmast and bowsprit were tensioned with a series of shrouds and stays. These shrouds and stays were of three-quarter-inch-diameter galvanized-wire cable with eye splices around thimbles, and were parceled and served with tar-soaked jute cloth and Russian-hemp marlin wrapped evenly and tightly to cover the splices. The stays, which ran fore and aft with the lay of the vessel, and shrouds, which ran perpendicular to the lay of the

THE MASTS AND BOWSPRIT of a swordfishing schooner, next to a
wharf at Gloucester, c. 1920. It is obviously a swordfisherman, with
a striker's stand at the end of the bowsprit, and standing boards
rigged in the foretopmast stays (the boards to support the crew
while looking for swordfish).

Sidney M. Chase photograph, Maine Maritime Museum

vessel, supported the bowsprit and the topmast and took the strain of any untoward weight which the wood by itself could not stand.

Coming down from the peak of the topmast there were two or three boards fitted upon which we would stand while looking for fish. The boards were spaced about six feet and a few inches apart. The outer edge of these boards had a notch to hold the foretopmast shrouds coming down on either side from the peak of the topmast, and they were lashed tightly, board and shroud together. The boards on the topmast grew in length as you descended. The center of the boards were indented on their after or rear side to fit the curve of the topmast, and heavy lashings secured the center of the board to the foretopmast.

There were ratlines (climbing ropes) lashed about every fifteen or sixteen inches to a shroud on one side and then the ratline was passed around the foretopmast in a clove hitch which was tightly seized. Then the ratline ran out to the shroud on the other side, where it was firmly lashed. The one-half-inch-diameter ratlines and the lashing lines were of tar-soaked Russian hemp.

The foretopmast was stayed off forward with a foretopmast stay that ran down from the peak of the mast and was fastened into a ring on the very end of the bowsprit. Another stay, the counterstay, ran from the rear top of the foretopmast back down to the hounds and spreaders of the main mast. All shrouds and stays were tightly adjusted so the rigging bore most of the strain, and not the wood of the topmast. All stays were tested frequently and adjusted by turnbuckles on deck to get the right balance of tensions. The port and starboard topmast shrouds ran from the peak of the foretopmast down through the outside of the foremast spreaders and then down to the foremast chainplates where the shrouds were fastened to the deck with a turnbuckle.

The crew was stationed on boards underneath the mastheadman. Generally the two crewmen with the best vision were on the board immediately under the mastheadman. The crewmen would stand on that board and be held by a canvas safety belt tied around the foretopmast and then passed around your butt and made fast by a safety clip to the appropriate foretopmast shroud, port or starboard. In addition, the crewmen were often enclosed in large wooden hoops much like the mast hoops that rode on the masts and were fastened to the luff of the schooner's foresail and mainsail. These were made of very hard, very tough woods, like ash or elm, that had been steamed and bent into hoops of about 24 inches in diameter. The ends were then overlapped and fastened each to the other with a set of copper rivets. The hoops were set at about belly height and were lashed on one side on the foretopmast shroud and then the other side was lashed to the foretopmast. Crewmen used to pad these hoops with strips of burlap so that your ribs didn't get chafed by the constant swaying and swinging of the vessel topmast as you fished. You wiggled your way up into the hoop when you got to your station on the topmast. The hoops and a safety belt made you secure, but it was a rare crewman who also didn't keep one hand on a shroud or an arm looped around the topmast for insurance.

Immediately below this first board was another which would hold two more crewmen. In bigger schooners there was even a third board. But the LORNA B, being somewhat smallish, had only the two boards which held four crewmen, and the mastheadman at the peak of the foretopmast. At the mastheadman station and at each other board on the foretopmast were pushbuttons for an electric horn which allowed the mastheadman to direct the vessel's course onto a finning swordfish. The signals were one blast starboard, one blast steady, two blasts port, three or four quick blasts to signal that it wasn't a fish, or that we had lost the fish. Upon receiving these signals, the helmsman would turn the vessel hard over in the direction indicated, port or starboard, as fast as he could go, and then immediately whip her back on course upon receiving the steady signal.

When a fish was spotted, the mastheadman would bring the vessel around in such a fashion as to always bring the striker, the harpooner, onto the fish downwind on a following sea, as much with the sun at his back as was possible. He would also watch the fish closely and if it were circling slowly, as finning swordfish oftentimes did, he would put the striker on the fish with the striker's cage, or striker's stand as we called it, just slightly to the right of the fish's circle if the striker were right-handed, or just slightly to the left if the striker were left-handed. If the fish was moving in a straight course, he maneuvered the schooner to put the striker dead on him.

It took a pretty good head to coolly assess these varying conditions and give the striker the best shot possible. If you went into the sun, or even if the sun were on the striker's side, the sunbeams and reflections on the water could blind him. At best he would be able to see only the fins and not the body of the fish; if it was what we called an underwater fish—one not finning—then the chances were he would see nothing. Harvey was a crack mastheadman. The one place where he was never irascible or excitable was when he was at the masthead of a swordfisherman.

The striker or harpooner was stationed at the end of a 15- to 20-foot-long bowsprit, whose exact length depended on an individual vessel's size. The bowsprit was tapered and was about 14 to 16 inches in diameter at the butt. This butt end was fastened onto wooden bitts on the main deck of the vessel close to the stem and then ran out through a hole just inside the vessel's forward bulwarks where they came together directly above the stem. The bowsprit was made fast inside at the bitts with a mortise-and-tenon arrangement.

The tapered bowsprit, when fitted and fastened, had a striker's or harpooner's stand on its forward end. The stand was composed of a 10-inch by 10-inch grate made of a galvanized iron. Attached to the grate were four thick galvanized rods which ran up to and were attached to a ring collar at waist height so as to support the striker's body securely on the stand. There were also rods of galvanized iron running back at an angle from the top of the stand down to the bowsprit, where they were bolted in place. This arrangement of rods stabilized and secured the

OF THESE SCHOONERS at a Gloucester wharf about 1920, the nearest one is seen to be a swordfisherman by the striker's stand and standing boards. Above the boards in her foretopmast rigging is dangling the mastheadman's seat, the position for the best spotter of swordfish.

Sidney M. Chase photograph, Maine Maritime Museum

stand from coming loose or rolling. The whole rig was like the pulpit on a modern yacht.

A bobstay ran down from underneath the striker's stand and was fastened to the vessel's stem at the waterline. The bowsprit had a port and starboard stay that ran in from the end of the bowsprit and was made fast at chainplates some 10 feet down from the bow of the vessel on either side. The bowsprit also had another stay of wire cable which ran down from the foremast spreaders to the tip of the bowsprit. Finally, the foretopmast stay ran down from the peak of the mast to the bowsprit tip as has been earlier described.

When you looked at a swordfisherman you saw her topmast and her bowsprit well supported by stays and shrouds that complemented and made even all of the stresses that could be put upon either the bowsprit or the topmast. There were lots of times, inadvertently, when the vessel would come up off a sea in rough weather and slam her bowsprit under water to a depth of as much as two fathoms, with the striker holding on for dear life, buried in the sea. There were other times when the vessels would take 30- to 35-degree rolls and more, with the topmast gang thinking they were bound straight for Fiddler's Green—but a stout vessel always righted herself. After such a roll, you giggled with relief and hoped that you hadn't peed in your long johns.

A one-inch-diameter Manila line was lashed to the foretopmast stay at the end of the center of the bowsprit and then ran in and was lashed again to the jib forestay running to the bowsprit. It then ran in at shoulder height along the bowsprit and was lashed again to the forestay on the vessels stem. The line was tensioned tight so that the striker could run in and out on the bowsprit holding the lifeline to balance himself in any kind of weather, fair or foul, that the vessel could fish. All possible surfaces that contained shackles and pins around the bowsprit and its stays were covered with canvas and stitched tight so that no wild loop of a slack buoy line could get caught and pull a harpooned fish off the dart.

A Doryman's Day

All that first day we worked to the east, hoping to see the silhouette of another swordfisherman, one from Nova Scotia or perhaps from Newfoundland. She'd be instantly recognizable by the long pretty sheerline that was the mark of a schooner's hull, by her bowsprit, and by the foretopmast sticking up into the air like an indignant finger pointing up to the heavens. We saw no one. The Bank was empty. We were alone.

Late in the afternoon we ironed one fish, hoisted the number-one dory overboard, and I jumped in to go out to haul the fish. Usually when a fish was harpooned it would immediately make for deep water, no matter in what depth it was harpooned.

It took a few minutes to get the first dory rigged and ready, and Jack said to me, "We'll tow you up." The buoy keg holding the line was already three or four hundred yards to the northward. I passed him the dory painter, and the vessel towed me up directly in line with the buoy and about forty yards in front of its course. I dropped off and coiled my bow painter. I next stuck the lance point up in the riser (an internal stringer that runs fore and aft along the dory's frames). I did the same with my gaff, making sure that both lance and gaff would be immediately behind and to the right of me when I started hauling. I rigged the tail strap open and ready to lasso the fish's tail when I had him. I placed the dory roller in the chock on the starboard gunwale well up into the dory's bow. The roller is a hardwood wheel with a grooved center that's used to haul a trawl longline or swordfish buoy line. It reduces friction and saves the wood of the dory's gunwale. Because of its placement, it keeps the dory well forward, bow up into the sea, as the doryman hauls. I then inserted my tholepins (oarlocks), got out the oars, and rowed to the buoy and gaffed it.

The buoy is placed in the eye of the dory so that when a swordfish is being hauled it is secure and out of the way. A second buoy line of 100-fathoms length is always coiled in the dory's stern, and the top end of this line is brought forward and immediately tied to the end of the first buoy line. The knot holding the first line onto the buoy strap is a slipsheet bend tied with the

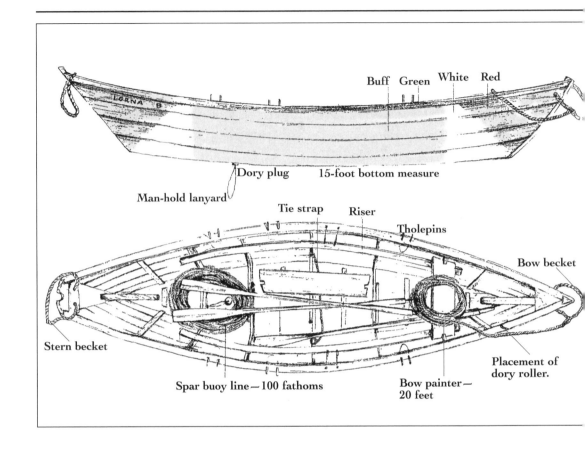

Buff Green White Red

Dory plug   15-foot bottom measure

Man-hold lanyard

Tie strap   Riser

Tholepins

Bow becket

Stern becket

Placement of
dory roller.

Spar buoy line — 100 fathoms

Bow painter —
20 feet

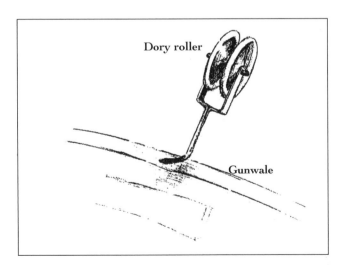

Dory roller

Gunwale

Above and right: illustrations by Jill Pridgeon

bight of the buoy line so that with one snap the doryman can untie the first line from the buoy and be feeding the reserve line overboard if the fish goes deep.

I began to haul while the LORNA B took off looking for more fish. Usually a swordfish will allow itself to be brought up fairly close to the dory without a great fight. You can almost always get the five-fathom mark in your hand, but then the swordfish spots the dory and begins a great sweep for the bottom. He goes down and down and down. The doryman can do nothing but take the line out of the roller, step a couple of steps back, so as to give the fish the drag of the full side of the dory against his course, and let out line gradually as he takes it. The line slips through your hands, which are covered by nippers. A nipper is a round ring of tightly rolled wool that is covered by a closely woven strong piece of cloth and then stitched tightly to make a deep groove in the center. You place the line in the center of this groove and wear the nippers on the fingers of your hand. With only a slight

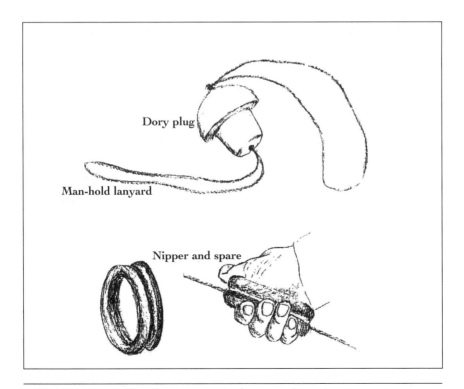

Dory plug

Man-hold lanyard

Nipper and spare

squeeze of your fingers, with the line between the two nippers, you can make a God-awful tight hold which will soon snub up any manner of beast.

The fish ran on me. He took out all the first 100-fathom line and then some 20 fathoms of the reserve line and then he stopped. He continued to fight for another five or six minutes, and then I began to gain line on him. The buoy line was passed once more into the groove of the roller on the starboard bow, and I began to make the rhythmical coils of line onto the bow thwart in front of me with my knees well braced against it. The line came steadily. Every once in a while there would be a flurry, a beat of his strong tail, and he would take a few coils. But each time I got a lot more back. Finally there was no movement on the line and I began to coil at greater speed. The coils mounted in a neat pile in front of me.

The five-fathom mark came through my hands and I leaned out over the side, looking for the fish as I continued to haul. He came to the dory with no struggle; he was dead. The pike or rod of the harpoon, with the dart fastened on its end, had driven in just behind his dorsal fin, down through his abdominal cavity, and passed out of his belly flesh just below the napes (collarbones). The fish was, as we said, "toggled." Alec had made a perfect hit. That tremendous dive the fish took and the resulting pressure of the great depth had forced great weights of water into his stomach from both holes, and the water had drowned him fast.

Nevertheless I lanced the fish through the gills until a good cloud of blood came out in the water. It was always best to bleed the fish. A fish not bled will leave blood in the blood vessels passing through the flesh, which always leaves a bitter taste. I quickly strapped the fish's tail after bringing it up with the gaff and tied the end of the strap line with a slip knot into a tie line that ran across the dory's bottom from a frame on one side of the dory to the other side. The tie line was an inch-diameter Manila line that had been spliced through the weep holes of the frames just aft of the dory's center. When the vessel came to pick you up, you could flip out the slip knot of the strap and still hold a good strain on its bitter end.

I tied the buoy line up close to the buoy, leaving slack from the five-fathom mark outside of the coils to the fish. You left this slack so that if the fish slipped off the strap or off the vessel's boarding tackle, you would have enough slack line to grab it and pull him back up. If the fish got totally away from you, and you lost the line, you still had the rest of the buoy line coiled and tied to the buoy so that you could easily pick the buoy and line up and retrieve the fish. Having the buoy line coiled neatly close to the buoy allows the buoy line to be used immediately once it is untied from the dart strap, which is in the fish.

I had come aboard and was slacking the painter of the dory aft. (Once on the ground, swordfishermen always had a dory out on the painter and tied to the stern.) I had just tied the dory up when someone aloft spotted another fish and immediately there were two blasts to port. The cook was on deck tending the buoy lines and buoy, and he yelled at me to get a quick cup of tea in the galley. For some reason Jack didn't like that and growled at me, "Feed your goddamn face tonight, not now." I stayed on deck, standing out of the way, by the mainmast shrouds.

Harvey had the vessel proceeding dead on course to the fish, which was quite a ways off. Alec, the striker, looked over his pole (harpoon) closely. He made sure the bib line was clear. The bib line is a line roughly 20 feet in length, running from the end of the harpoon back to the striker's stand where it is tied off. The purpose of the bib line is to retrieve the pole after a shot. Next Alec checked the dart to see that it was fitted tight on the lily or the rod at the other end of the harpoon. The harpoons were some 15 to 18 feet long, depending upon the striker's size or preference. The poles were tough, straight, round pieces of ash, somewhat limber, of $2\frac{1}{2}$ inches in diameter. The dart was tied into a short strap which was a loop of $\frac{1}{4}$-inch-diameter Manila hemp. The straps were some 15 to 18 inches long. The straps were made up by passing a 3-foot length of line through the hole in the center

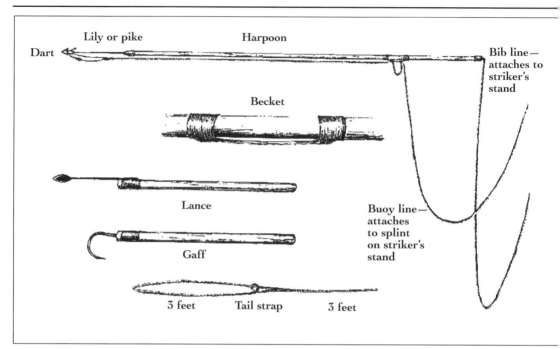

Above and right: illustrations by Jill Pridgeon

of the dart. Then the two ends were spliced together with a crown knot on each side of the splice and then three tucks on each side. The dart itself was made of bronze and was $4\frac{3}{4}$ inches long, $2\frac{1}{4}$ inches wide. The front of it had a head like an arrow and the point and edges were very, very sharp. In back of this arrow point was another arrow-headed shape, but its edges were dull, and the rear of it curved up and away from the main line of the dart. When the dart was punched into a fish, the drag of the line would exert pressure onto the dart and the rear curved blades of the dart would turn into a position where the dart would lie solidly embedded and perpendicular to the strap in the flesh of the fish.

Alec checked the knot that tied the buoy line to the strap. This too was a single slipsheet bend. The buoy line ran down his pole to a hardwood becket of some six inches in length that was taped onto the harpoon some three feet from the end. A bight, or a half loop, of buoy line would be run through between the hardwood becket and the pole, and the bight would be cinched tightly in place. Alec then payed out a bight of about fifteen to sixteen feet that ran in front of the bib line and up to another hardwood becket at the starboard side of the striker's stand. A bight of line was fed into this becket and then the buoy line would run in along the bowsprit and outside of all the rigging to a position just aft of the foremast shrouds. The 100-fathom coils and the buoy would be laid out neatly and ready with the bight of the line tied with a slip knot, securing the buoy line and the buoy to the shrouds to prevent their being carried over the side

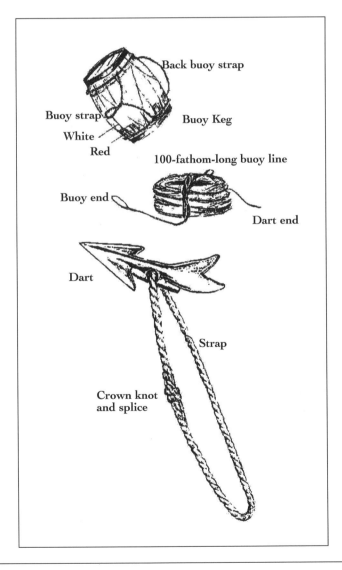

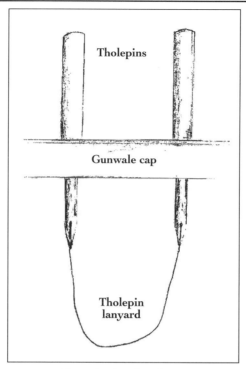

Illustration by Jill Pridgeon

in rough weather. Tending the buoy line was the cook's responsibility. He would pile out on deck whenever he heard the mastheadman's horn.

We came up on the fish, Harvey blowing very few signals, very much in command. As we neared the fish, Alec stood up and balanced his pole. He swung his shoulders a little bit, working out whatever muscle kinks there might be. He swung his right leg back, bracing it against one of the back legs of the stand. He raised the pole, pointed the tip up over the horizon, and in one easy movement he gradually lowered it down, sighting along the pole to the fish's back. And then—with his whole body—he lunged, hitting the fish at a distance of about fifteen feet in front of the bowsprit stand. It was the finest kind of a hit. The fish's tail threw white water and the buoy line whipped out of the becket on his pole, snapped out of the becket on the striker's stand, and Nathan hauled slack for dear life.

A Doryman's Day

Simultaneously, Jack threw the wheel hard to starboard so as to clear the line from the vessel's side, while at the instant the fish was struck the engineer threw the engine out of gear to stop the propeller, lessening any chance that the propeller would cut the buoy line if the fish ran hard to port and under the boat.

As soon as Nathan had taken in all the slack and saw that the rapidly turning vessel had sent the line well off to the starboard side, he threw the coils of buoy line and buoy over the side. The buoy and quite a bit of line remained on top of the water as I ran aft and jumped into the dory, yelling at Jack to let go the painter. I could still see slack line on top of the water. I could get to the buoy with no more than a few strokes of the oars.

I was alongside the buoy in a quick spit and gaffed it. After shipping the oars into the dory, I set the buoy again up in the bow. As I started to haul, the vessel came by and Jack yelled that he wanted to go off ten or fifteen miles to the west. It was late in the day by then, and I could hear Nathan say to him, "Jack, mind the light, there not be much daylight left." Nathan turned and yelled, "Do you have a torch in the dory, boy?" He was referring to the kerosene lamps that the dory fishermen used when long-line trawling. I replied, "No." He then said, "It's a grand supper I've got tonight. Haul your fish now, boy. We won't be far, will we, Jack?" Jack gave him a black look.

I laid on and started to haul the fish. He came easier than the first one did. I got him up and he only went down about forty or fifty fathoms before he began to swim in circles, struggling a bit now and then. I soon got him right up to the dory, but I was very cautious, being afraid of a "puncher." A puncher is a swordfish that doesn't act like all the rest. He may stay very close to the surface rather than going down. He may turn and run along the floating buoy line, following it like it was the road to destruction, and then smash through the side of the dory with his sword. Or sometimes a fish would swim in circles under the dory and then all of a sudden he would turn his head and bolt for the dory's bottom. It was not a regular thing, having punchers break you up, but it happened often enough so that dorymen were very leery about fish that didn't behave the way they should once they'd been harpooned.

In the summer of 1947, when I'd been in the schooner JORGINA SILVEIRA, a fish had punched me and split the whole bow of the dory with his sword. He started to slat with his sword and laid open the leg of my oilpants, boot, and clothes, and gave me a good gash. The dory had sunk with the swordfish stuck in the bow and I could do nothing but lie down, holding onto the buoy keg in the water. The fish had gotten a bad cut in the gill from a splintered dory plank and there was a cloud of blood in the water. All I could think of was sharks. The vessel got up to me fast, brought me aboard first, and then salvaged the fish and the buoy line. They got the oars and the other gear out of the dory and then let the rest go. The dory was nothing but scrap wood, her bow demolished.

But hell, if I were a fish and I'd been harpooned and was fighting for my life, I surer than Jesus wouldn't behave the way whoever had hold of me thought I should behave. I'd have cut the lights out of the son of a bitch hauling on me. I'd cross him up and punch him, if I were the fish.

I looked at the fish carefully when I got him up. The one clear sign you have that the fish isn't going to give you any more trouble lies in his color. When swordfish are alive, their backs and the top of their sides are of the most brilliant, gorgeous, rich purple that has ever been seen by anyone. Their sides and their bellies are the silver of freshly minted coins. They are so beautiful that there is a small part of you that would like just to look at them and see them in all their royalty and then let them go in peace. But there's another bigger part of you that says, "This is your living. Killing is a necessary part of it." That little voice in you says, "Quit jerking around, boy. Haul the fish up. Lance him." A dead fish is easily known. The purple back has turned to a deep-black-chocolate color and the sides and belly are a dirty grey. This fish was dead, so I bled and strapped him, tied my buoy lines, and looked for the vessel.

I could just make her out a long way out to the west'rd. I thought it best if I rolled the fish into the dory and started rowing for the vessel. It would cut a little distance off and besides, I did not want gannets (voracious seabirds that never cease feeding—this was the term that we called each other if we thought the other fellow had an overabundant appetite) to get not only their share of Nathan's supper but mine.

I tied the fish's tail high in the forward part of the dory and pulled his sword up by the buoy line as I walked aft. I got my gaff into the outside gill cover, stretched his body along the dory gunwale, put my knees down on the dory gunwale, and rolled down with my body, while at the same time lifting the fish's head with the gaff. I wrapped my right arm over the base of his sword, and then rolled backward with my body, levering back and heaving inboard on the fish's head and his sword. He rolled and thunked down into the bottom of the dory. Sometimes with a big fish you have to strap the buoy keg under the gunwale of the dory's side to give you some buoyancy when rolling the big fish in. If you try to roll too big a fish into the dory, her gunwale will go under water and you may ship a great deal of water.

I coiled my painter over the roller, unshipped the oars, and began to row for the vessel. All I had to do was keep the dory's shadow straight astern in the lowering sun and I was on course. I kept rowing along and enjoyed it. It was a good workout. I loved to row, loved the discipline and the precision of the movements, loved snapping my wrists down to feather the blades when they were out of the water and horizontal, parallel to the water, with my body rolling forward to take the next stroke. I liked the sound of the oars thunking and creaking in the tholepins and loved seeing the little drops run down and off the blades of the oars when they came out of the water, making a series of minute arrows with their wakes as they hit the water. I looked around several times, and the schooner was bearing down on me. It was apparent they had found no fish. Harvey, Willy, Manuel de Pinto, and the other two Portuguese were still up on the "stick," looking as long as any light lasted.

The vessel came down on me, picked up my painter, and we hoisted the fish aboard. The sword of this one and his predecessor had been cut off the minute they hit the deck. The engineer sluiced their bodies down with the washdown hose and he covered them with wet burlap sacks and a canvas to keep them cool until they were dressed after supper. Nobody said much. Two fish for all day. It wasn't a very good start. I probably wasn't the only one who tossed it over in his mind that maybe we'd been a little bit too prideful and dumb in thinking that we could wiggle another trip out of this season.

But we went down to supper, and as usual it was a good one. Nathan had made a bean soup. He had roasted a couple of chickens with oven-browned potatoes and some more corn. We had to eat it up, you know. He had also made a Lad in the Bag. This is a favorite dessert of Newfoundlanders. It is a duff pudding which is steamed in a cheesecloth. It's loaded with pieces of dates and raisins and quinces, and they make a hard sauce with it that you cut with a knife rather than spooning. The hard sauce is something that brings a smile to the face of any Newfoundlander—it's made with Demerara rum. Jack wouldn't eat it. He growled about alcohol and about all those who partook of it. He said, "No more goddamn alcohol is going to pass my lips," adding, "I'm only sorry that I have to ship with people who still drink."

None of us bothered to answer except for Harvey, who said, "Jack boy, since you're not going to eat your ration of sauce, would you be kind enough to give it to me, old son." Jack growled, "No, I'll give it to no man. Throw it out." Harvey retorted, "You're a terrible man, Jack, a terrible man. It must be hard to live with yourself." At which point Nathan interrupted, "The both of you shut up or you can get out of the fo'c's'le and you'll get no more grub from me."

A Doryman's Day

We went on deck and dressed the fish. Dressing the sword-fish is a pretty intricate proposition. The tail and all of the fins are sliced off neatly. The gill covers are pulled up and extended and cuts are made to sever all connective tissue between the nape or the collarbone of the fish around the gill and back down to the lower jaw. The same is done on the other side. All of the gills and the gill tissues are now cut clear of the fish. Next the head is chopped off about six inches in back of the eye. The fish is then rolled onto his back and a slice is made from the anus in a straight line up to just below the napes, taking care not to penetrate the stomach and the entrails. The knife is then taken inside the collarbones and the connective tissue is worked loose. The anus is then cut out and all of the entrails are worked up and out between the collarbones. Next a connective tissue called "sweet meat" has to be scraped out carefully from the abdominal walls with a knife designed especially for that purpose. Then the kidney or backbone blood is cut out and the backbone is carefully scraped to get rid of as much blood as possible. Following this, the insides of the abdominal cavities and the corrugations along the backbone are scrubbed out with brushes, burlap, and salt until not a speck of the blood or the "sweet meat" remains. The insides of the abdominal cavity are smooth and clean. The fish is then washed thoroughly, strapped, and placed in the hold for icing.

The days that followed were much like that first day. Good weather, fine weather to see fish, no boats to keep us company, not much sign of fish. We managed to get only one to three fish a day. Long doleful days passed with little to do on the masthead except scan from horizon to horizon, in and out from the vessel, looking for a quick flicker of fins cutting the water or the royal purple of a fish meandering along just under the surface.

Our eyes were getting burned. Every morning now, we washed them out with boric acid solution and again before we slept. We rubbed our fingers on the flues of the galley stove pipe to get soot in our fingers which we carefully painted below our eyes, so that the sea glare might be cut. The constant sun and breeze dried and chapped and cut our lips. We all had lip sores, and nothing to put on them but Vaseline. It smarted now, when you ate soup or drank a hot cup of tea or coffee.

On the fifth night we ran across the bank some eighty-five to ninety miles to the Southeast Part of George's. The place was a Christly desert—no birds, no sign of life, no bait, not even a shark's fin, let alone a swordfish. We had blown a day and steamed back that night to the Northern Edge, with nothing to show for it.

On the seventh day, Jack came up out of the cabin with the shotgun and he shot a pair of gannets who had come in to pick at the spoils of Nathan's slop bucket bobbing in our wake. Gannets are wild, free birds of the open ocean who glide effortlessly on the updraft of the wind and who dive like a dive bomber upon bait that they see ten, fifteen, twenty feet below the surface of the water. They can fly underwater—they have such strength—with wingspans of close to five feet. Their wingtops are black and barred and underneath the bird is snowy white, except for his yellow eyes and his yellow curved beak and yellow feet. The birds lay dead on the surface, broken, blood on their snowy white vests, and the wing of one of them cracked back and broken.

We all looked down on deck, horrified. Willy began to cry. No sound, just tears rolling down his cheeks. The Portuguese crossed themselves, and Harvey began to swear a string of invectives at Jack. Nathan stomped aft and said to Jack, in a very heavy voice, "Give me the gun, Jack. You're all done shootin'. You don't need to take it out on God's other creatures." Jack handed him the gun. We continued to fish. We ran for another six or seven hours, in and out, back and forth. But no fish. I grew very uneasy. I couldn't help but think then of the Ancient Mariner and the albatross.

We had now been out ten days. The trip was more than half over. We had twenty fish. At this rate, we'd have close to a "broker" and the scupper-mouthed wags of Gloucester would be proven right. There were no trips to be had in the month of October on the Northern Edge of George's Bank.

We had a somber supper. Nobody talked much. Even Harvey was quiet. We finished up and Jack left the table to go aft and get his bearings on the radio direction finder. We settled around the table, drinking a second mug of tea and having a smoke, all of us with the long empty stare that comes to fishermen whose luck has run out.

Suddenly—Bang! Bang! A foot was kicking the doghouse that shielded the companionway that led from the deck down into the galley. And then a roar, "You cold-coddled canker-headed Jesus, you and your old man, you're a pair of towel-headed Arabs! I'll take either one of you on! Come down on deck and fight like a man, you slimy-sided sons of syphilitic angels! I'll drag you from this vessel stem to stern and I'll kick in your goddamn ribs!" Jack then kicked the doghouse again and yelled down at us, "See how you like them apples, you Bible-whackers!"

We were absolutely stunned. None of us had ever heard anything like that. I don't know how religious the rest of us were, but I knew the Portuguese were. Manuel had told the other two the gist of what Jack was saying and they were all kissing their crucifixes and their religious medals which they wore around their necks, and making the sign of the cross. Willy didn't have a smile. He just sat looking down between his knees. Nathan could only say, "Oh, Jack boy. How have you gone wrong? What is it that is into you?" I didn't say a word. Harvey sat with his head thrown back, and very quietly said, "Jack, you're a real package. You're bad enough so's you'd f--k up a free feed at the Last Supper."

After a bit, Jack went aft again. This went on for the next two nights. He would come forward after supper, kick the doghouse, and yell again at God, denouncing Him, and daring Him to come down on deck and fight like a man. By this time, all three of the Portuguese would dive for their bunks as soon as Jack opened up.

I have never in my some seventy years heard such blasphemous and outrageous talk come out of a man at sea. The third night Harvey said, "There, boys, is the Flying Dutchman, in all his agony and in all his hate and in all his fear. He's cursed, he is."

Jack let loose again. "You camel whallopers, get your asses down here and by the spit-whiskered cold-cocked Arabian Jesus, I'll drive you into the deck until your jawbones break your feet. You ain't big enough to take me on, and you know it. You're hiding your slimy asses behind the clouds." He then went aft.

The next day we only got one fish, and the engineer had him dressed before we came off the masthead.

Before Jack came forward that night, Nathan said to me and Manuel, "Boys, we've got to stop that man. Now here's what I want you to do. Barry, you get up forward of the doghouse before Jack comes forward. It'll be dark by then. Take the shotgun—she's loaded—and take this dishpan and this big ladle with you. Manuel, you take my big white tablecloth with you into the top dory and hang there out of sight in the bow, which is right alongside the doghouse. Now when Jack comes forward, let him kick the doghouse and get raving good, and Barry, you fire off both barrels of the shotgun well up over his head, but not too far. Grab the dishpan and the ladle and bang them together and scream like a banshee. Manuel, at the same time, hold the sheet up in the air in front of you, yell like hell, and jump square onto that son of a bitch's back and cover him with the white cloth. Get it around his noggin if you can. The rest of the crew and I'll stand around the ladder and moan and groan like the souls caught in the last hinges of Hell."

Jack came forward. He kicked the doghouse two or three times and started in again. "God, I'm tired of waiting. You ain't got the guts nor the balls to take me on. You're a fiddle finger, that's what you are, and you run the biggest bluff going. Come down here on deck and I'll bounce your goddamn Nubian head off every stanchion on this vessel from stem to stern, and then I'll heave your crab-bitten old carcass overboard."

At just that point, I fired both barrels of the shotgun. Bam! Bam! Sheets of flame went up ten feet into the air. I no sooner had the ladle and the dishpan in my hands, banging them together and screaming, than Manuel landed square on the old bastard's back, driving him down to the deck and wrapping him up in the cloth. And then came this godawful chorus of moans and groans and screams from the fo'c's'le. It sounded lots worse than I had imagined it would.

Old Jack rolled around on the deck, with Manuel on top of him, and I was whacking away with ladle and dishpan as close as I could get. By this time, the rest of the gang had piled out on deck and we couldn't help it, we started to laugh. Jack broke free and ran, screaming, aft. That old bastard broke the world's record for the 40-foot dash, which was the distance between the dog house and the cabin companionway. The rest of us were right after him. Leading the pack was Harvey, hollering, "The bear is bound for his cave! The bear is bound for his cave!" Nathan came next, swinging both arms high up next to his chest, like a champion long-distance walker. The Portuguese, Will, and I trailed behind.

We piled into the cabin and there was Jack, in his bunk, head under the pillow, with both his quilt and his blanket pulled up over him. We all laughed and snickered until Nathan said, "That's enough now, boys. Go forward and turn in. Which one of ya has got the first watch?"

We went forward, feeling a hell of a lot better. Jack couldn't even take on a bunch of fishermen, let alone God. The three Portuguese said a prayer of thanksgiving, or at least that's what I think they did. There was a lot of cross kissing and genuflecting going on.

The night passed easy. We were still blessed with good weather. In the morning Nathan called all hands to breakfast, but Jack wouldn't come forward. Nathan went aft, and said, "Breakfast, Jack. You like breakfast, Jack. And it's good for you. We got sausages, and salt codfish hash, and eggs, and pancakes. Besides, I fixed the porridge just the way you like it, with some cinnamon and brown sugar. Come on, Jack. Get out of the bunk, boy. The boys will not say a word about what happened last night. We got to finish the trip, Jack. And you're the boy that's got to lead us. You're the skipper, ain't you, Jack? Come forward and eat your breakfast." But Jack stayed in his bunk, limp, almost like the life had been driven out of him.

After awhile, Jack came forward. He sat down and ate. Nobody said a word about last night, last week, or a hundred years ago. We did make sure that all the breakfast fixings were close at hand to Jack, the sugar, the canned milk, salt and pepper, and a bowl of raisins. We knew Jack liked raisins. We had finished breakfast and were having a smoke and a second cup of coffee. Jack laid right into the grub. We might have scared the shit out of him, but it didn't bother his appetite any.

Just about the time he finished, Nathan yelled from the deck where he was standing watch, "Fish! Fish! There's a big son of a whore finning right alongside of us!" Everybody made a mad dash up the companionway. Like any vessel's companionway, the ladder is narrow and only one guy can go up or down at a time, normally. That morning on the schooner LORNA B, there was two and three guys at a time come squirting up that ladder and out onto the deck. The engineer in his greasy overalls went charging aft to start 'er up. Harvey was runnin' up the rigging and pulling on his oilskins as he went. Two of the Portuguese were bound up the other side. Alec was already on the bow, untying his pole. We all saw the fish. It was a big one.

Jack was smart and waited for the fish to swim off a ways, so we could throw the engine in gear and get ready and come down on him without spooking him. After a few minutes with the gang all in place, Jack gave the signal to throw her in gear.

We slipped up away from the fish, turned a good circle, and Harvey guided the vessel right onto the fish, giving Alec a beautiful shot. He nailed him, the buoy line snapped clear, and the coils of buoy line were going overboard. I ran for the dory but something made me run down forward and grab a water bottle and throw some hardtack into a sack before I went running aft to man the dory.

They dropped me off to haul. I soon had the buoy and began to work the fish. The vessel was fairly close and all of a sudden Manuel yelled, "There's another one, port!" One of the other Portuguese yelled, "Peix! Peix [fish, fish]!" It was another one. And then Willy yelled, "Oh dear God, there's another one dead astern of us!" I knew I was right in grabbing the water and the hardtack. Oh God! It might be a long day.

It was one of those slick, calm, clear days where sea and sky edges blended. You could see forever. Sounds were magnified because there was no wind to steal them away. The sky was blue, with just a haze of mist.

The vessel went round and round and round. Bang! They got the second fish. Bang! They got the third fish. Jack slowed her to drop another dory with Joaquin, one of the Portuguese, aboard when Harvey yelled, "Fish, dead ahead!" She charged down on that one and got him, too. Then they dropped another dory, with Manuel at the oars. By this time I had the first fish back and had rolled him into the dory and was rowing for a second buoy.

The vessel took a tack off to the east'ard and I could see her wheeling around four or five miles away. She was on fish there, too. I got to the second buoy and had no trouble with the second fish. It had already drowned. I rolled him into the dory, lashed the buoy lines, and started to row for two or three buoys that I thought I saw off to the north.

By this time the vessel was charging on down to us, and Manuel was on his second fish. The vessel came up to me at a good clip. I strapped the first fish and sent him aboard. I caught Jack's eye at the helm. To this day, I don't know what made me do it. But I yelled at him, "Hallelujah! Praise the Lord!"

That got everybody's attention. Nathan looked at me. Alec was peering in from the striker's stand. And the whole gang on the masthead were looking down at me in the dory.

Jack turned the black side of his face to me, and said, "You sassy young son of a bitch!"

Nathan heard some of it, and said, "Jack, what did you say to the young fella?" Jack looked at him and said, "I told him to go forward and get a cold dish."

That day we had three dories out working fish. I was in the first dory, Joaquin in the second dory, and Manuel in the third. We ironed, hauled, and killed twenty-three prime swordfish. At the end of it, I rowed up to the vessel when it was almost pitch dark, and only a faint line of lavender in the western sky, with two fish in the dory and one hanging off the stern.

It was a very happy vessel that night. Right in front of Jack, all three Portuguese thanked God for giving us a good day. Jack turned around and stomped aft, but he didn't say anything.

After a late supper we started dressing the fish. We had to break out the ice from three pens in the vessel's hold to stow the day's catch. When a vessel goes swordfishing, she fills the entire hold with ice, except for one of her fifteen or eighteen pens, which is left half-full. For the first few days of the trip, the dressed fish are shoved in on top of the ice and under the ceiling or overhead of the deck. When you have eight or nine fish, you have to break the hold out. This involves wiggling on your belly over the ice down in the hold and shifting ice from the half-empty pen after it has been chopped up. The ice is then shifted into the other pens with pushers, all around in the void between the top of the ice and the ceiling, all over the hold. You then shovel about a solid eighteen inches of ice on the bottom of the empty pen and then lay in the fish, head to tail and tail to head, until you've covered the bottom of the pen with a layer of fish. Small blocks of ice are cut to stick into the fish's napes so they won't be broken, and you ram ice with your booted feet into the abdominal cavity. You then jam ice in between the fish with your booted feet. And, finally, you cover the tier with about another ten inches of ice. You continue to lay tiers of fish and ice into the pen until it is full. Then you start on another pen.

TWO MAINE SWORDFISHING SCHOONERS taking ice for a trip, at
Horse Island Harbor (now Sebasco), c. 1905. The nearer schooner
is probably the BERNIE AND BESSIE of Portland. Both vessels have
the striker stands and boards to support lookouts.

George S. Graves photograph, Maine Maritime Museum

We now had forty-three fish on the vessel and we were up pretty late getting them dressed and down, but the deck was a happy place. Harvey was teasing Willy about girls in England and France. Manuel and I were joking about Portuguese bull-fights and baseball. The engineer told us some funny stories about a mule his father had who constantly farted in the old man's face while he was plowing. Nathan kept passing up little snacks of this and that. Jack was nowhere to be seen.

Before breakfast the next morning Nathan, who had the last watch, started yelling, "Two fish alongside! Two fish! Two fish!" We all came piling out of the bunks and darted up on deck, half asleep. Alec went running out on the bowsprit in his stockinged feet. Harvey managed to get up to the first horn station on the foremast crosstrees, and we went on the fish. While we were getting dressed and slurping down a quick coffee, those two fish were well ironed and the buoys were dancing away, off to the north.

Jack yelled for everybody to go aloft but Nathan said, "Let 'em get a bit of tucker in their guts, boy. They got to eat." Jack replied with little grace, "Okay." We all ran below to the table and grabbed what was ready, greasy bacon, half-cooked porridge, some slices of bread, and we were off. I packed some bread, a banana, and two handfuls of raisins in a sack, grabbed a water bottle, and ran aft for the dory.

Before the sun was well up, we not only had those two fish but another two ironed. We had two dories out, and we could see the vessel turning and working on fish just inside us. By one o'clock in the afternoon, the third dory was set and we went on through the day. As soon as we got one fish on board, another one or two fish were ironed. We ate in snatches. Nathan passed me a big bowl of stew when I came alongside with three fish. Again, when Jack looked at me, I yelled, "Praise Jesus!" Well, by this time everybody else had picked it up. The Portuguese, when they came alongside, were yelling, "Munte obrigado a Deus! [many thanks to God]" and "Jesus Maria y os Santos [Jesus, Mary, and the Saints]." Willy let fly with, "Oh, Lord, you are the way!"

and "Oh, God, you are our pilot!" Each time a fish was boarded, Jack was getting bombarded with Jesus freaks from every side.

The one that really tore it, though, was at about four in the afternoon, when we had better than twenty fish aboard, with Harvey singing out from the peak of the topmast, "Jack, Jack me boy." We looked up and here was Harvey, with only one hand wrapped around his safety belt, his feet on the board. He was leaning out at a 45-degree angle some 80 feet in the air, swinging with the roll of the vessel from the masthead peak and out over the void down to the deck, smiling, and waving his hat with his free hand.

"It surely is, Jack, it surely is! Washed in the blood of the lamb be we, Jack! Washed in the blood of the lamb and God's grace!"

Jack didn't acknowledge it at all. He gave me a dirty look and said, "Get your ass in the dory. There's fish out there to haul." Nathan came running up with a sack of doughnuts and a full water bottle and said, "Here, Barry, rear back on them fish and pull them so fast that they'll jump one hundred feet out of the water. You're the boy to haul, me son. You are a doryman."

We were giggling, Nathan and I. And then Nathan said, "Jack, steer a straight course. Look at the wake behind you, boy. Like a drunken snake with a broken back!" Again, no response out of Jack. Just a dirty look.

On that day, we finished late, too. Twenty-four fish. And now, no matter what happened, we had a trip. Not a big trip, but a trip that was worthwhile.

It continued on like that through the fourth day and the fifth day, the dories out soon after sunup, fish coming aboard all through the day. As each fish was boarded someone would yell, "Oh sweet Jesus, oh Lord, we thank you. Please God," etc., etc.

What had started as religious statements—perhaps just to counter Jack's blasphemies—were now becoming true expressions of thanks. Somebody up there was taking care of us. There were now lots of smiles and jokes and tomfoolin' around. Jack had lost some of his black look. He began to talk with us just like a skipper does when things are goin' good—giving words of praise for our skill and our efforts.

We ate good at each supper and then went on deck to dress and ice the fish. We finished up late at night, but now each night we took time for a hand or two of cribbage, or a couple of games of checkers. The engineer was a sneaky bastard. That black streak of grease didn't say much, but he could whump the bejesus out of any of us at checkers, crib, whist, or red dog. I don't think he had spent all his time looking at the ass of a mule in Missouri.

The next morning brought darn good weather again, but with a slight breeze out of the north. And there was a chill to it. It was the kind of wind that sneaks up the sleeves of your oilskin jacket and your heavy wool shirts and wiggles underneath your long-john sleeve, and you feel it going into the bone. It was late. And we knew it. Soon now George's Bank would be lashed by wintry gales. There would be times in the winter when the flying spray would stick all over a fishing vessel's sides, hull, rigging, and pilot house and form ice, ice that could build so thick on a vessel's topside that it would make her top-heavy enough to roll over unless you kept beating the ice off with wooden mauls and shoveled it over the side.

We had a couple of fish ironed soon after we started up and by afternoon we had twenty-one or two aboard. Then, all of a sudden, the action died when slack water came at the turn of the tides. The ocean was blank. We saw nothing. The birds had disappeared. The fish had disappeared.

And then in every direction, between the vessel and the horizon, from all points of the compass, you could see three or four or five swordfish jumping! Fish jump when they're coming on or leaving the bank. Nobody knows what this means. But they do it. It makes no sense to try to chase jumpers. They jump and they'll fin wildly for thirty seconds or a minute, and then down they go. We went on jumper after jumper, not able to get the vessel on one. Finally Jack yelled up into the rigging, "Come down, boys. Come down. I think she's all over."

We came down off the mast and Alec came in from the bow. We stood all in a cluster in the waist of the vessel and watched the fish jump. Oh, they were beautiful. They jumped up out of the water, ten to twelve feet clear of the surface, into the air. They seemed to hang in a curve, with those beautiful colors, silver and purple, poised vividly against a gray sea. What a quick sketch they were, outlined against the sky! And then, crash, down they'd go, back to the sea in an explosion of foam. We watched them for a long time. I've never seen a sight to equal that. We were all very quiet, just watching.

Finally, Willy stepped over to the rail and started waving his hand. "Good bye, fish!" he yelled. "Thanks for lettin' us take some of you. And to the rest of you guys, good luck."

The Portuguese muttered some words of thanks, too. Jack came up and knocked Nathan in the ribs and said, "I guess we done her again. We got a trip." Lord God he was right! We had a trip. Counting what we'd taken that morning, we had one hundred twenty-eight fish on the vessel. A fine trip in any year, and by far the best one in 1948. The fish were going, the wind picked up, and it was blowing ever colder. Jack told the engineer to start her up. We cleared the dories from the stern and hoisted them aboard, one dory inside the other, snug and done for another year. Jack swung the vessel off to the west. We were bound for home.

We dressed the fish and put them down and iced them all handsomely. We turned in early that day and just ran through the skein of watches on into the evening. Nathan called us for supper and there wasn't too much to eat. We were just about out of grub. We had been out twenty-two days. He had caught a couple of big hake with his meat line the night before. A meat line was a fish line with two or three hooks and a lead on it that you set to drag on the bottom to get a codfish or two or maybe a couple of haddock to eat.

Nathan did have an onion and some tomato sauce and, with

the fish, he made a soup. We also were eating the last of Nathan's good bread. As we were drinking the soup, Manuel said, "In Portugal we eat a soup like this, just fish and a little flavoring, and it is called the Soup of Sorrows. What that means is that when you drink it, you think of all who you have known and who aren't with you anymore. You also drink it for those who are still alive and you drink it with the hope that you and they will still be alive next year to fish and to drink the soup again."

Jack said, "That's a fine thought, Manuel. I'll never eat fish soup again but what I'll think of you and them words."

We went through the night, standing watch by watch. The cold was getting to us and in the middle of the night, for about two hours, the northern lights painted the northern sky with waves and shards of green, silver, and faint purple.

In the morning we began to scrub the vessel down. We washed and then flaked out all the buoy lines into loose coils for drying. Alec cut the straps out of all the swordfish darts and strung them all together on a bit of line. The dories were washed. All the buoys, some thirty-eight of them, were washed and lashed against the port rail forward and aft of the dories. We made up soft straps from strands of inch-diameter Manila line to unload the fish. Alec cut the bib lines from the poles and lashed them all together in a bundle on the mainmast port shrouds. We dorymen did the same with the lances and the gaffs, putting them into the top dory.

By the time we had finished this work, we were abeam of the tip of Cape Cod and now it was only two and a half hours to the Boston Fish Pier. When you come back from a long trip like that, especially one as lonely as ours had been, you can feel the approach of the land sometimes better than you can see it. The sky to the west looked different. (We now call it smog.) You begin to see more garbage on the surface of the water. The seabirds seemed different. There were no more gannets to be seen. No more Mother Carey's Chickens. They are also birds of the ocean deep.

We began to see the buildings of Boston on the horizon. The Old Customs House first. At that time the Customs House was the tallest building in Boston.

We made the Boston Lightship abeam and stood up by Deer Island and then Castle Island coming up the south passage toward the Fish Pier. We took down and furled the sails and lashed them snugly into the gaskets. When we tied the vessel up at the pier, it was late in the afternoon and there were only a few souls around. A couple of them said, "How many fish do you have, Cap?" After a long pause, Jack said, "Me and the boys got a hundred and twenty-eight fish, the finest kind. They're Northern Edge fish."

The engineer stayed aboard the vessel as a watchman and the rest of us went up on Atlantic Avenue to get some supper. I remember it as being pretty good, but nowhere near like the grub Nathan dished out. We came back to the vessel and turned in. At 6:00 AM Jack had had his coffee and had gone up to the auction room at the end of the Fish Pier. He had posted the vessel's name up on the sales board. "The LORNA B of Gloucester, one hundred and twenty-eight swordfish from the Northern Edge of George's."

Only a few of the fish buyers knew that we had been out. But with that posting every goddamn thief of a fish buyer came running to the auction room. We had to stay on the vessel. Crewmen were not allowed in the auction room. We walked up and down the deck, smoking cigarettes and drinking coffee and eating those greasy sickly sweet doughnuts that the mug-up wagons lug around. We were hoping for a price. The last trips had gotten anywhere from fifty-five to sixty cents a pound. We were dreaming of maybe seventy-five or eighty cents, since it was the last trip of the year. We didn't dare to push our luck; even if we got no more than sixty cents, we still had a hell of a trip. I don't think we could have put more than another seven or eight fish into the vessel. It was a grand trip.

After awhile, Jack came walking down the dock with his head thrown back. He came up to us, all of us there in a ring on the dock. I can still, over the span of fifty years, see his face so clearly. There were spikes of silver-white hair sticking out from under his swordfish cap, whose bill was split and battered because of too many anxious tugs of his hands during the last three weeks. I can still see that deep blue of his eyes, like a break in the clouds when a winter nor'wester sweeps through. I can still see that walnut-hued face with all the deep creases of laugh lines and squint lines carved by wind and water and sun. Oh God, I can still see the big grin on his face so that every tooth in his Sears Roebuck-guaranteed top and bottom plates was shining like a tropical pearl.

He looked around at us, and he looked at the sky, and then he grabbed me with one arm and Willy with the other and said, "Boys, we got a dollar eight a pound." And then he looked up again and yelled, "Praise the Lord!"

We were shocked at that pronouncement, but not enough to prevent us from proceeding to pile around and on him, hugging him and each other and laughing our goddamn fool heads off.

Then Jack said, "Now boys, let's get with it. We got to get these fish out, such as they are. Most of us got women waiting for us." And he looked at me and said, "Even though some of us have got women waiting for us that we don't know about yet and neither do the females yet."

We began to swing into the rigging to board the vessel. We had hired two lumpers (longshoremen) to shovel out the ice as we discharged the fish. I was walking forward to rig the takeout line when I heard these two in a terrible argument, screaming and swearing at each other.

From up on the dock, Jack bellowed down, "Avast with that swearing and them profane words. You she-maggots, you burnt barbecue-fingered Satan scum, no bad words on this vessel." And he looked at us and grinned. And then he yelled, "This be a Christian vessel!"

There was a crowd around the boat up on the dock all day long looking at this gang of fools who'd snatched a big trip out of a foul season. They were drooling over the amount of money that one hundred and twenty-eight fish at the price of one dollar eight cents a pound represented. I'll admit, we probably showed off a little bit before them. I was chewing on a whacking great Cuban cigar a fish buyer had given me.

The fish came swaying up out of the hold and landed on a wooden pallet one by one. Will and I sluiced them out with water and wiped them down with burlap to get rid of the slime and any ice clinging to them. Their color now was a dirty dove-gray on the backs and an off-white on the bellies. It was hard to think of them as once having swum in great color, the top predator of the sea.

Jack and the fish buyers' representatives tallied the weight as each one crossed the scale. They marked the weights, each on his own card, and confirmed what each fish weighed to each other.

When the load was about half out, Willy said to us, "It's cruel, cruel to think of how easy these poor animals come out when they died so hard and we worked so hard to get 'em."

Jack replied, "I know, Will. I used to cry when I first went fishing with my dad for cod in the traps down home in Newfoundland. The codfish would come aboard and gasp in the boat and their mouths be open, and it was more than I could stand."

By noontime, the vessel was empty and her hold and the pen boards had been scrubbed. And, as is always true, in a place where fish are bought and sold, when the last fish come out of you, the buyers and the other shore sharks lose interest in you. They don't notice you again until you've got another trip to sell.

Jack's wife had come down to the Fish Pier to ride to Gloucester with us. We helped her aboard the vessel and she took up her perch, sitting on top of my pillow on the top of a buoy keg right by Jack at the wheelbox. She was quite a plump woman with a handsome face and a good smile. She knew some of us but wanted to be introduced to everybody and thanked each one of us for helping Jack. She said, "No fish is caught by a captain alone. Thank you, boys."

Nathan had bummed a couple of haddock and from a friend who was a cook aboard a Boston trawler, got some potatoes and onions and salt pork and a couple of gallons of milk and some hardtack and made a grand fish chowder.

We ate the chowder and then laid around the deck as we made the passage from Boston up to the east-northeast to Gloucester. Several of us offered to stand a wheel trick for Jack but he said, "No. I've been standing for three weeks now, boys, and I want to stand a little longer at this one's wheel."

He stood back there, one hand on the spoke of the wheel, with his jaw stuck up in the air. Mrs. Brant had brought him his fine summer Panama straw hat and he was wearing it even in the chill of late October. There they were together, Jack with one hand on the wheel and the other one on her shoulder, or holding her hand.

We went on home to Gloucester, passed up into the harbor, and Jack slowed the vessel down. As we began to thread our way through the inner harbor, little Harvey was standing up in the nest of the dories. The rest of us were standing on the rail hanging onto the shrouds or we were perched on the lower ratlines of the rigging watching the boats.

The harbor was full that day. There were vessels laying two and three abreast at every dock. Lots of people waved at us. They all knew by now of the trip we had had. Two or three vessels began to blow their horns and, as we went up into the harbor, we were saluted by everybody. Those same sons of bitches who'd called us "misfits in a junk pile of a boat" three weeks before were now friendly-like. Not many of us felt like answering their greetings. As we passed five or six vessels laying abreast at one dock, Harvey couldn't restrain himself any longer.

He stood up in that top dory and yelled at them, "Here boys, take a gander at this!" And with that he flipped off his suspenders, turned around, dropped his pants, and mooned the whole goddamn town! That was bad enough, but then he yelled, "You can all line up in front of City Hall at high noon to kiss my rosy-red Newfoundland ass!"

Jack was laughing, but he told Harvey, "Harvey, mind your place. There's a lady aboard." Harvey answered, "Sorry, Mum. I forgot." Mrs. Brant yelled back, "Harvey, me son, I never saw a thing. What are you talking about?"

We brought the vessel into the dock and tied her up. The owner was waiting and I had never seen a man who acted more "delivered" than did he. He was laughing and crying. He had enough money to buy the winches for the vessel and a hell of a lot more besides.

We had grossed somewhere over $24,500 for the trip. In those days that was a fortune. Seventy-five dollars a week was a big wage for a working man in 1948. Each man was gonna get somewhere between $1,650 to $1,750, plus we had over $200 a man in swordfish-liver money.

The owner had some cash for us, $100 a man. We'd receive our settlement and our shares for the trip the following day. None of us was going dragging in the vessel, so we had our bedrolls and seabags packed, and we started up off the dock. Jack said goodbye to us as we left the vessel and he shook our hands and thanked us, one by one.

We got up off the dock and there were taxis waiting. Alec said, "Well, let's go have a goodbye drink." The owner said, "I'll buy the first round."

Nathan said, "No, boys, she's over. Let the trip and the vessel rest. It's been fine knowing all of ya, but I have to get home and see how the horses and the dogs have been making out at the track. Well done, young fellas, well done."

We shook each other's hands and mumbled a goodbye, or "It's been good to have been shipmates with you." The three Portuguese piled into a cab next, and then Willy and Alec and I were left. I knew better than to tell Alec to stay off the sauce. I turned around for one last look at the vessel and she was there and Jack and his wife were walking slow-like up off the dock holding hands.

A horn blew and I turned around. My dad was there in the car to pick me up. "So long, Alec, so long. See you, Willy. It's been grand." I turned and waved at Jack, and got a wave back. I got into my dad's car and went home.

❊ ❊ ❊

I never saw Jack Brant again. He went back to Boston. He never got a swordfish vessel to command again because of his age. About all he could get after that was a fill-in trip here or there on a Boston trawler as a mate. He was an old man. He died the second year I was in Korea, in 1951.

Nathan Foot lived a good long time. He quit going cook on fishing vessels at the age of seventy-six. He was a bachelor and kept a spic-and-span apartment in Dorchester. He played the dogs and the horses and was a steady patron of the track. On fine days in the spring, summer, and fall, Nathan would ride the subway into Boston Center and sit in the Public Gardens among the flowers, working out the bets and odds from the racetrack newspapers and magazines he had. He died peacefully in his sleep when he was eighty-one.

The engineer, a couple of years after our trip, went back to Missouri for a visit and never came back. I guess he stayed there, happy. I guess all them goddamn mules had died or had been re-placed by tractors. The farms were making money again.

Manuel de Pinto told me, when I saw him many years later, that he and the other two Portuguese had made out pretty well. Manuel had invested his money as a partner with another Por-tuguese fisherman in a boat. They did pretty well until Manuel wanted a dragger of his own, which he bought and then skip-pered out of New Bedford, chasing black-back and yellowtail flounder. John had fished for about ten more years in America. He had saved his money, and had gone back to Portugal and bought a small farm. The other Portuguese, Joaquin, continued to fish out of New Bedford. He married and had a small family and a flower garden and he loved all of them.

Willy turned out well. That winter after our big trip his brother Donald sent over to England for the English girl that Willy had been courting before he went to war. He paid her passage over and she took charge of Willy. They lived together for three months and then they married. Over the years they had four lovely daughters. The family love loosened Willy up a bit and he had a good life. He never got to be a captain. He didn't want the responsibility of running a vessel and commanding a crew of men. But he was a good hand and had the best of jobs on vessels out of Gloucester. Donald told me that one of the best sights in the world was to see the daughters come down to greet Willy when he came home from a trip. Donald said that, "You could see the face of heaven when you looked at Willy and his girls."

Alec froze to death in the winter of 1949. They found his body in an alley by a barroom. The coroner's report said there had been a great deal of alcohol in his system. The coroner had no need to say that last. Alec was a great striker. He never missed a fish. He had hit 128 in a row and every one of them square on, right in the middle of the swordfishes' backs, that October on the schooner LORNA B.

Poor Harvey keeled over dead of a heart attack right into a checker pen full of fish on the deck of a Boston trawler two years later. Harvey had been a pretty frugal man, and between his investments and his life insurance, he left enough so his wife could buy a small home in New Hampshire and live well.

And me? I went a'roving. I've fished in four oceans and four seas. I've had to fight two wars in my life, which I and the world could have done without. I've fished with men of many nationalities and colors and with men who did not worship the same God as I do. I've fished with canoe men in the far southwest Pacific and the Philippine Seas. I've fished with live bait and pole for tuna out of Palau in the far west Pacific. I've fished with Scots and Norwegians, chasing the herring down in the Minch of the Hebrides Islands and in the North Sea. I've fished with sailing sloops in the Caribbean, dory fishermen out of Boston and Nova

Scotia, draggers in the North Atlantic, swordfishermen, scallopers, purse seiners before the power block and purse seiners after the power block, I've fished pots and traps, and I've trolled for salmon and for tuna. I've fished with bottom and mid-water trawl all along the Pacific Coast and into the distant Bering Sea.

I also went to a great university after my army service in Korea. While I was in school, I married a lovely redhead, a talented practitioner of the dance: ballet, jazz, and modern. We had two sons, who are now happily married. My youngest grandson says they are successes: "They are both married, they both got jobs, and they ain't in jail." My loved one has part gentled and civilized me. In turn, I think I helped brace her up some so that she became a good inspired teacher and a lady independent in her ways who has done a lot of good in this world. On all the nights I passed at sea and away from her, I missed her presence. But on the nights that we've spent together, over some forty-five years, I've recognized through her what it is to be whole.

And in all these places and with all these men, I've learned that a man's value is not in his skin color or whatever god he worships but rather in what he can do for himself, but only after caring first for the vessel he's in and for the men with whom he has sailed as a shipmate.

As I write this it's been fifty years now to the month since that trip on the schooner LORNA B. What I treasure most is that for one great week we were a grand company of men led by a great skipper in a vessel that didn't let us down. We taught each other a lot. We were for that short time what Gloucestermen—vessels and men—were all about. We were damn fools but, like the Sicilian fishermen say, "God takes care of the crazy ones, the damn fools."

The Vessels

MARJORIE PARKER

According to *Merchant Vessels of the United States*, an annual publication of the United States Treasury Department, Bureau of Customs, the MARJORIE PARKER was built in 1923 at Essex, Massachusetts. She was schooner-rigged, as you can see from the photographs published herein, but she had engine power from her beginning: first a gasoline engine, later (by the time of Barry's story) a diesel. She measured 76 gross tons, register length 78.3 feet, breadth 21.7 feet, and usually carried 17 fishermen. Barry said that when he was aboard they had 10 or 11 dories and thus a total crew of 20–22 plus cook, engineer, and captain. Her first home port was Boston; by the late 1940s she was owned by the Portland Fish Co. in Maine, and her home port was Gloucester. In the early 1950s her home port became Portland, Maine, and on August 31, 1954, she foundered at Fairhaven, Massachusetts.

ROBERTSON II

The ROBERTSON II was a Canadian vessel, and our information is a bit skimpier. She was built in 1940 at Shelburne, Nova Scotia, and fished from there for many years. When her fishing career ended, she was sold (about 1974) to the Sail and Life Training Society (SALTS). SALTS brought her through the Panama Canal to Victoria, British Columbia, and adapted her to be a sail training vessel. She provided active sail training programs for young people until being retired in 1995. She is still operated by SALTS for younger trainees, but does not leave her wharf. According to information provided by SALTS and the American Sail Training Association, the ROBERTSON II measures 170 gross tons, length on deck 105 feet, breadth 22 feet, one inch. She also is diesel-powered but schooner-rigged, and once had a complement of about 20 fishermen.

JORGINA SILVEIRA

This vessel was built as a schooner, but with a 100-horsepower diesel engine (later upgraded) from the beginning. She was built at Essex, by A. D. Story, and may have been a Thomas F. McManus design. Measuring 62 gross tons, her register dimensions were length 74.7 feet, and breadth 19.6 feet. She normally carried a crew of 10. Barry went swordfishing in her, but most of the time she went dragging. In 1958 her name was changed to the J.B.N., although her home port was Gloucester throughout her career. On March 28, 1975, the J.B.N. was destroyed by a storm approximately 40 miles southeast from Eastern Point Light, which marks the entrance to the outer harbor at Gloucester.

LORNA B

The LORNA B seems to be a fictitious name. The reader is welcome to look her up, but we found no such American vessel in the years around 1948. In a preface to an early version of "Mysterious Ways of the Lord," Barry said, "This tale is based upon truths. All of the events described here were true happenings. I have changed some names and dates to protect the virtue of the innocents and to 'hide the misdeeds of the guilty.'" There may be some relationship with the JORGINA SILVEIRA.

Information on the vessels supplied by Nathan R. Lipfert, Maine Maritime Museum.